Only The Dog Knows For Sure

The Best of
THUH
BULL

The World's Worst Newspaper Since 1991

LONGSTREET PRESS
Atlanta, Georgia

Published by LONGSTREET PRESS, INC.,
a subsidiary of Cox Newspapers,
a subsidiary of Cox Enterprises, Inc.
2140 Newmarket Parkway
Suite 122
Marietta, Georgia 30067

Printed in the United States of America

1st printing, 1997

Library of Congress Catalog Number: 96-79803

ISBN: 1-56352-391-4

This book was printed by Quebecor/Kingsport, Tennessee

Only The Dog Knows For Sure

The Best of

THUH

BULL

The World's Worst Newspaper Since 1991

A bout 6$^1/_2$ years ago I was bankrupt and needed money to buy such insignificant little things as food and shelter, and such very significant things as rot-gut scotch. My Dad and I were sitting in a Hardee's restaurant when I had an idea. We went to Hardee's because my Dad could save eight cents on a cup of coffee with his senior citizen discount. The local shopper had just come out and everybody in the joint was reading about used cats and backhoes for sale. I told my Dad, "Darn, if people will read this crap, I bet they would read funny crap, too, . . . with a few ads thrown in along the way to help pay the bills (and to buy rot-gut scotch)."

So, to make a short story even longer, I went to fourteen advertisers and offered them a no-lose proposition: "Let me put an ad in the Bull newspaper and if you get a good response, pay me for the ad. If not, you don't owe me a penny and I'll go out and get a real job." Well, thirteen out of the fourteen got good responses, paid me, and the rest, as they say, is history. This book contains what is arguably the best of the first six years of the Bull newspaper. If this one sells well, we'll publish another one and argue that *it* really contains the best stuff. In the meantime, enjoy.

—Bobby Weaver

DEDICATION

To my late Dad, P-38 fighter pilot in WWII and best friend . . . and to the 3rd best Mom in the world. I don't who the first and second best moms were, but they must have been damn, I mean darn, good ones.

ACKNOWLEDGMENTS

Ron and Kathy Smith . . . *world class graphics and production*
Peggy Nichols . . . *BULL typist*
Kren Holzapfel . . . *I really haven't figured out what he does*
Graham Evans . . . *ditto*
"Honest Hal" Bullard . . . *cartoonist and full-time redneck*
Chris Wilson (*You can pick your friends, you can pick your nose, but you can't wipe Chris on the couch.*)
Jack Seay
John Dean
Roy Centanni (*the Rude Dude*)
Bob and Diane Elko
Steve Enoch (*my favorite agent*)
Bob Delozier
Scott Coffman (*worst golfer on the planet*)
Robert Backe
Fred and Judy Garner (*Mr. Farking Bastage*)
Bernie Richey
Dave Kocker (*killer cartoonist*)
Tammy Smith
Crossan & Crossan Creative
Chuck Clark
Mark York
Dave Claus

Doug Lurie
John Baldysh
Robin White (*wild woman*)
Bo Neman
Mike Morris
Ed Severson
Mark and Lisa Mayberry "16.3"
Greg Nolan

and many other contributors and friends too numerous to mention

A SPECIAL THANKS

This goes to Jim Paige and Joy Anderson of "THUH Florida BULL" in Jacksonville/Orlando. If it weren't for Jim's story about the "Prom Queen" this book might never have happened.

Lifestyle

Madonna to undergo
"virginity transplant"

Doctors at John Hopkins say that there is a 99% chance her body will reject it.

USA
WHENEVER
P O L L

Over 93% of the people in Georgia who saw the movie "Apollo 13" did not understand it. When asked why, most respondents said, "Because we didn't see the first 12."

Setting the record
S T R A I G H T

Contrary to our report yesterday, that's a man and not Barbara Bush on the front of the oatmeal box.

BULL'S 2ND ANNUAL
COLLEGE FOOTBALL'S
TOP **5** RECRUITING PICKS

❶ Bubba "Onion-Breath" Batson: Defensive Linebacker. Played out of Bill's High School, Opp, Alabama. 385 lbs. of pure athletic ability, yet intellectually bankrupt. I.Q. hovers at or around that of plant life. Once won the Alabama State Tire Eating Championship. Can recognize a football with little or no help from others. Has been know to stop an ugly freight train with his speeding face. Majoring in Remedial Art. Hobbies include bench pressing his Uncle's doublewide and wandering. Hopes to join the College Hunting Team.

❷ Rufus "Hubcap" Washington: Defensive End. Played out of Raford State Prison. 234 pounds and can run the 3-minute mile in about 58 seconds. He practices running in the off-season with nothing at all but the help of a few pursuing patrol cars. Has never been arrested on a Tuesday. Rufus is a very, very dark-skinned African-American. In fact, his coach was quoted as saying, "Rufus is so black that every time he runs by my car, the oil light comes on." Majoring in Criminal Defense.

❸ X Smith: Right Tackle. Played out of a major Correspondence School out West. 399 lbs. of dumb. Yes, X ain't real smart, but you sure can say one thing about him — he's stupid too. But to be fair, you hand him a football with a good set of instructions printed on the side and he can play with the best of them. Majoring in P.E. with an emphasis on litter control after a home-coming game. Hobbies include walking, then sitting down and chewing gum, then walking, then. . . .

❹ John "Chokehold" Poindexter: Left Guard. Played out of Mosley High School (which, by the way, almost won one game in a row last year) in Panama City, Florida. 486 pounds. Only son of Tom Poindexter, owner and co-founder of that world-famous pork flavored ice cream, Hog N Daz. Got his nickname from accidentally strangling to death 37 of his classmates for making fun of his last name. Very heavily recruited by *Unsolved Mysteries* and the *FBI*. Majoring in Food. Hobbies include eating big seven-course meals in between little fifteen-course snacks.

❺ Tyrone (Tyrone doesn't know his last name but he's narrowed down the list of suspects to Jones, Simpson, Smith, Williams and a couple of Washingtons): Special Teams. Played out of Leroy's High School in the Bronx. 170 lbs. or 205 lbs., depending on whether he's got somebody's car battery with him. Used to have a drug problem. In fact, during one game last year he mistakenly snorted the entire 50-yard-line. Much to his credit though, coaches like the fact that Tyrone has cut his hubcap stealing during half-time down to an absolute minimum. Tyrone has never missed a starting lineup, unfortunately, over half of those were at police stations. Majoring in Pharmacy. Hobbies include spending quality time with his probation officer.

A CLASSIC LETTER

Dear Dad,
   I mi$$ you. Gue$$ what I need the mo$t? Plea$e $end it $oon.

                   $incerely,
                   Your $on $teve

Dear Steve,
   We kNOw you love us. I got your letter at NOon today. Write aNOther letter with your grades. If they are good eNOugh, everything will be as YESterday.

                   Your Dad,
                   NOel ReYES

Great books start with great first sentences

"There I was, sitting in a maximum security prison doing 15 years to life for not rewinding a tape from Blockbuster Video. . . ."

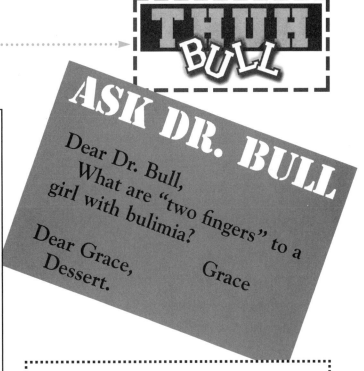

THUH BULL

ASK DR. BULL

Dear Dr. Bull,
What are "two fingers" to a girl with bulimia?
                   Grace

Dear Grace,
Dessert.

For a reprint of this article see below.
For a reprint of this article see above.

WHAT'S THIS?

Thanks to "Honest Hal" Bullard for this and many other ridiculous cartoons in this book.

ANSWER: *Pinocchio's aborted brother.*

continued from the front cover
"so they left."

A day in the life of a
ROACH

5:50 a.m.: "Oh, it's been a long night and I'm tired. I think I'll hit the underside of a refrigerator early today."

6:00 a.m.: Hide

9:00 a.m.: Hide

3:00 p.m.: Hide

6:00 p.m.: Hide

9:00 p.m.: "Wow, I slept great. I feel like a new roach. Time to get up and get crawling."

9:12 p.m.: "I wish these jerks would hurry up and go to bed. I hate those bright lights."

10:31 p.m.: "Thank goodness, the news is over and it's lights out at the Jones' house."

10:32 p.m.: "Oh wow, a nice crumb of dog food. I wish Orkin made dog food. This Purina crap has no taste whatsoever."

11:51 p.m.: "Goodie gum drops. I hear someone getting up for a glass of milk. Maybe I can scare them into a full cardiac arrest. I hope it's not that stupid kid that likes bugs."

11:52 p.m.: "Oh great, it's the Mom. This will be fun."

11:54 p.m.: "Okay, here goes — around the light bulb, over her foot, off the dish drainer, nothing but milk!"

11:55 p.m.: "Wow! This is better than causing a heart attack! She's gonna feed me some Raid. I love it when a plan comes together!"

12:30 a.m.: "You know, roach life is the best. You're not part of the food chain, you normally have the kitchen all to yourself and, thanks to Orkin and Raid, our life expectancy has increased 78% in just the last 5 years."

3:27 a.m.: "Yes! Someone is coming again. I'll just lay here on my back next to the oven and play sick. Then some nice family member will gently pick me up with a paper towel and put me in the garbage can. You think Raid is good, you ought to try Mrs. Jones' tuna casserole. It's horrible, I love it."

5:17 a.m.: "Well, I suppose it's time to head for crack sweet crack under the oven."

5:30 a.m.: "Good night, John roach."

HeyBull!

What's the difference between a beer and a booger?

Hey Booger Fan!

The beer goes on the top of the table.

Bull History Lesson

What did Dan Quayle say when he was asked to spell 'Mississippi'?

"The state or the river?"

☛ **THIS JUST IN**

The First National Bank of Poland opened last week and offered each customer $500 if they brought in a *toaster*.

---

3 Things to say to an old person
(To cheer them up)

1. If you painted yourself purple, you could go trick or treating as a raisin.

2. Don't you think you should start buying your calendar one month at a time?

3. You need some new transportation don't you? I'll take you shopping today and you can kick the tires on a few used wheelchairs.

It's the 90's

Q: How do they end nursery rhymes in the 90's?
A: ". . . and they lived happily for quite some time."

LEWIS GRIZZARD ON EDITING

Lewis shown here reading the Bull.

. . . had a senior editor in Chicago who bragged he could edit the entire *New Testament* into one paragraph. He did it for me:

"He was born. He lived. He died. He's coming back and he's not going to be real happy."
. . . Auter, former edit . . .

THUH BULL

BULL
T-SHIRT
OF THE MONTH

WHAT'S THIS?

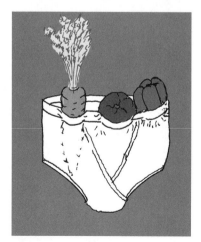

VEGGIES OF THE LOOM

Dear Bull,
  What two words are you most unlikely to hear together . . . "Romantic Battlefields" or "Anorexic Hogs"?

          Mark L.

Dear Mark,
  Neither! The two words you have not and never will hear together are "Sergeant" and "Clinton".

The Truth About Punctuation Marks
(Full-color photos too)

THE MOST BORING BOOK IN THE WORLD

ONLY THE DOG

KNOWS FOR SURE

THINGS I FOUND IN MY WIFE'S PURSE

1. All the usual stuff. You know, combs, keys, lipstick and a table saw.

Plus:

2. Another purse
3. Thirty-seven dollars and nineteen cents worth of hamster food coupons
4. A hand-held rear view mirror
5. Seven years worth of pocket change
6. Three decomposed crackers
7. 40 percent of a postage stamp
8. Two dead batteries in a new flashlight
9. A green thing
10. Two tickets to last year's something
11. A one-leafed clover
12. A nice inventory of Bic ballpoint pens
13. One broken tampon
14. Six napkins and some toilet paper decorated with lipstick smears
15. A "Sorry you missed another PTA meeting" note
16. Half of a complete set of shoe strings
17. Four half-melted birthday candles
18. About a half a cup of sugar (or possibly salt)
19. What was, at one time, probably a lemon
20. The remote control we lost 7 months ago
21. A bottle of "New Purse" air freshener
22. And 18,000 other things

P.S. All of the above list is true except, of course, for the table saw. Everybody knows you can't get a table saw in a purse; it was a car battery.

WHAT IS THIS?

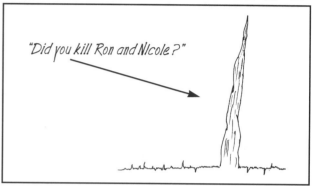

"Did you kill Ron and Nicole?"

Answer: It was recently reported that O.J. took a lie-detector test 2 days after the murders. He did great except when they asked him (above) "Did you kill Ron and Nicole?" His answer was such a lie it went off the chart. Lie detectors are not admissible in a California court of law. Simpson scored a 'minus six' on the test. (True) To put that in perspective, when Bill Clinton said, "I didn't inhale," he scored a 'minus two.'

2 UNABOMBER FACTOIDS

☞ The Unabomber started off his career innocently enough. He told investigators, "I'll never forget the joy and thrill I experienced one Christmas Eve when I sent my Grandmother a gift-wrapped cherry bomb. You should have seen the delight in my eyes when it blew off her little wrinkled fingers."

☞ Nothing personal, but I really think I would prefer a letter from the Unabomber to another one from Publisher's Clearing House.

DR. BULL'S

HOME REMEDIES

PROBLEM	REMEDY
Bad breath	Don't brush after every meal, brush after every sentence.
Dry skin	Get a job skin-diving for Roto-Rooter.
Broken leg	Right after you break it, head to K-mart. Don't forget to take a banana peel with you. Your leg could be worth up to $70,000 in cash and prizes.
Dry eyes	Have a loved-one volunteer for a plane crash.
Depression	Suicide.
Dark circles under the eyes	Put a lemon under your eye. If that doesn't work, move to Africa.
Dandruff	Watch three Head & Shoulders commercials and then call me in the morning.
Chicken pox	Grow up.
Cataracts	Don't grow up.
Bee stings	Scream as loud as you can for 3 hours and like magic, the pain will go away.
Tennis elbow	Checkers, perhaps.
Sunburn	Seattle.
Stuttering	Vow of silence.
Snoring	Sleep deprivation.
Low blood pressure	Hire a local serial killer to chase you around your living room with a butcher knife.
Belching	Try something new, *manners*, for instance.

BULL JEOPARDY

ADVERTISING	SCIENCE	SPORTS	MISC. B.S.	FOOD
Pizza Hut spends more on this one item than it does on the entire rest of the pizza $200	The most common ingredient in a box of grain cereal. $200	What a batter does when he has 4 balls $200	The best thing about Jim Carrey's film "Cable Guy" $200	When ordering a cup of McDonalds coffee, you get these at no extra charge. $200
Made the slogan "you deserve a break today," world famous $400	What 9 out of 10 doctors should recommend $400	In golf, it's called a '0' $400	On April 15, an estimated 35 million Americans do this at the last minute $600	At McDonalds, this original menu item is still only 49¢ $400
Valu-Jet now advertises itself as "the safest airline in the world" $600	What millions of Americans fight to prevent at the bathroom sink every morning $600	A very exciting, action packed spectator sport $600	**DAILY DOUBLE** The swine flu.	At a famous ice cream chain, you can find 31 of these $600
The two words Wal-Mart uses that appeal to millions of patriotic Americans $800	Main reason Alexander Graham Bell wishes he had never invented the telephone $800	If you enjoy seeing this, by all means drive up through South Carolina in the Fall. $800	**If you at home would like to appear on THUH BULL JEOPARDY IN-HOME Sweepstakes here's all you do:** Send us your Clue and Answer to: Bull Jeopardy Sweeepstakes Box 4191 Panama City, FL 32401	
Marlboro Lights are said to have less tar than this $1,000	These destroy more mobile home communities than any other force of nature. $1,000	During the Opening Ceremonies, Americans would have stood and cheered if they heard this $1,000	If we select your entry for our next "Double Jeopardy" round, you win a Bull T-Shirt and a chance to become a finalist on our Final Jeopardy Contest coming up in a few months. P.S. That winner gets big bucks!	

ANSWERS ON NEXT PAGE

BULL JEOPARDY

ADVERTISING	SCIENCE	SPORTS	MISC. B.S.	FOOD
What is "the box they're delivered in?" $200	What is a "three day supply of air?" $200	What is "pay twice as much as everyone else for a vasectomy?" $200	What is "the popcorn at the concession stand?" $200	What are "third degree burns?" $200
Who is "Tonya Harding?" $400	What is "that other doctor?" $400	What is "the score a cheater writes on his score card when he gets a hole-in-one?" $400	What is "cheat on their taxes?" $600	What is "a small cup of ice water?" $400
What is "because we're grounded?" $600	What are "bad hair days?" $600	What is "anything but bowling?" $600	**DAILY DOUBLE** How did Bill Clinton get from Arkansas to Washington?	What are "fat pigs standing in line?" $600
What is "Kmart sucks?" $800	Who is "Mrs. Alexander Graham Bell?" $800	What are "pathetic football teams?" $800	**Subscribe to Thuh Bull now and don't miss a single round of Jeopardy!!** Subscription form on inside back cover	
What is "a five-mile stretch of Interstate 65?" $1,000	What are "the residents that live there?" $1,000	What is "that the plane carrying the Russian Track and Field Team just hit the side of a mountain?" $1,000		

ANSWERS

Blonde Classifieds

03 YARD SALES

Big yard sale this Saturday morning. 301 Lane Ave. Beautiful 80' x 12' yard for sale. Just mowed. Will include the sprinkler system.

If you already have a yard, this sale is for you. It's a garage sale. It used to be a kitchen but my husband converted it into a beautiful 3 bedroom, 2 bath garage. Shown by appt. only. Please call for my telephone number.

35 LOST & FOUND

Lost: $20,000 diamond studded necklace in the vicinity of someone's backseat. Reward. Oh, nevermind, I just found it.

Found: Last month I found a one hundred dollar bill. I placed a classified ad. 374 people called to claim it. I had to mortgage my home to pay them all. Please stop calling my unpublished number which is 813-9162 or my office number which is 813-2214.

Dear Bull,
What did you call it when your ex-wife and 3 daughters spent an entire day at the mall?

Clark C.

Dear Clark,
A jump-start to the national economy.

Dear Bull,
You once named the **"10 Best Ways to Get Kicked Out Of Disney World."** What was number one?

Bill J.

Dear Bill,
I can't remember; it was either driving down Main Street, USA with Bambi's mother strapped to your fender or taunting the guy in the Pluto costume for not being able to find a better job.

WHAT'S THIS?

CURIOSITY

QUESTION CURRENT EVENTS TEST

All of the facts in the questions are true. See if you can pick the real answer instead of the B.S. answer we made up.

1. UPS may start carrying passengers on its under-utilized weekend flights. What you might see or hear . . .

A. "Excuse me sir, would you like to sit on a window box or an aisle box?"
B. Beautiful young stewardesses in horrible brown uniforms.
C. "Folks, this is your Captain, we're a little short handed today, so if you don't mind, how about helping our crew smash a few of the packages marked 'fragile'?"

2. What did female astronaut Shannon Lucid say to her mother on May 12th, 1996, from the Russian space station, Mir?

A. "Happy Mother's Day, Mom!"
B. "Mom, guess what? I just joined the 200 Mile High Club!"
C. "Oh, by the way, there's a frisbee on your roof."

3. The FDA just approved a new microwave device for use in the treatment of prostate cancer. But what you don't know is . . .

A. It only works if your prostate is the size of a 7-11 burrito.
B. It is not very effective, for some reason, on women.
C. Actually, the main problem is that your prostate gets hot on the outside, yet stays cold in the middle.

THE SHADOW NEVER LIES

"Where do y'all get off calling me a Mickey Mouse President?"

BULL
Birthday Notices

Tom Arnold is 37. You talk about talented, Tom has more talent in the tip of his finger than most actors do in their entire thumb!

Willard Scott recently turned 62. His hair is 13. His other hair is 9.

MURDER
INSURANCE FOR KIDS???

USA Today reported last week that many families in New York City's crime-ridden neighborhood were buying murder insurance on their kids. The Bull Research Team was there when Mrs. Alice Jefferson called to inquire about murder insurance for her son.

Mrs. Jefferson (MJ): "Hello, I need a little murder insurance on my boy Willie."

Insurance Salesman (IS): "Why, of course you do. Where do you live Mrs. Jefferson?"

(MJ): "In the Bronx."

(IS): "Oh, goodness this might be a tough one. I'll need to ask you a few questions. First, look out your window and tell me what you see right now."

(MJ): "Well, right now it's pretty quiet. Let's see now, the bakery across the street is being robbed, only 2 dudes are bleeding to death due to multiple stab wounds, and other than a couple of gang rapes in progress, it reminds me of a Sunday morning. I wish all days were like this."

(IS): "How many children do you have?"

(MJ): "Well, when I first moved here 3 months ago, I had six, but now I'm down to just Willie."

(IS): "Is Willie in good health?"

(MJ): "Other than the stray bullet lodged in his right thigh, he is."

(IS): "Tell me Mrs. Jefferson, does Willie go out at night?"

(MJ): "Well, occasionally I used to take him out to watch the drive-by shootings and get some ice cream, but right now our armored personnel carrier is in the shop."

(IS): "Well, Mrs. Jefferson, I have some good news and some bad news. The good news is that we will sell you $10,000 worth of murder insurance on Willie."

(MJ): "That's wonderful, what's the bad news?"

(IS): "It will cost you $11,000 — up front."

(MJ): "Heck, that is a lot cheaper than what Allstate quoted. I tell you what, Willie just went to take out the garbage. If he makes it back in okay, I'll call you back and we'll do the deal."

(IS): "Willie takes out the garbage in THAT neighborhood! — Click

FORGET  GERBER

BULL INTRODUCES
GOOBER
for Redneck Babies Everywhere

☞ THIS JUST IN

Thuh Bull hereby forms an association for the "Elimination of Exclamation Points." Our membership will consist of people that are no longer surprised by anything.

...

The smartest blonde in the world was asked by the Bull to invent something to prove blondes aren't stupid. Well, 3 years and 15 minutes later she did it. She calls her new invention a solar powered flashlight.

BULL FACTOID

☞ If 'Clinton' is the answer, it must have been a stupid question.

My most embarrassing pick-up attempt

I spotted a lovely young sweet thing at a local nightclub the other night and decided to use my power, popularity and high community standing to pick her up. I walked over to her and said, "Bull, Thuh Bull." She looked up, smiled and said, "Dead. Drop dead."

I WOULD DO THE SAME FREAKIN' THING!

Two men on death row were scheduled for back-to-back executions. On the appointed day, the warden asked each if he had a last request. "Yes, sir," the first said, "I'd really like to hear Achy Breaky Heart one last time." "And you?" the warden asked the other. "Please," the second condemned man pleaded, "kill me first!"

RAISE YOUR STUPID LITTLE HAND

That's right, raise your hand if you agree that the speaker boxes at drive-thru hamburger joints really bite the big one! You can't understand a word they say, so how the heck can they understand you? Last week, as a test, I went up to the drive-thru at McDonalds. When the voice came over the speaker, (I have to assume that they were asking for my order) I read 3 verses out of the book of Genesis. Sure enough, when I got finished, the order taker said, "Your order comes to $14.37. . . please pull forward."

More compassionate, lovely little letters to THUH BULL

Imagine my surprise when every time I read these stupid letters you always use the phrase 'imagine my surprise.' Fortunately, I always see the funny side because I have never read your stupid paper in the first place.

Last month my husband was having a terrible pain in his right leg. Imagine our surprise when the doctor diagnosed the problem as terminal. Fortunately, we finally saw the funny side when it dawned on us that Herbert had a wooden leg and the doctor hadn't said terminal at all, he said *termites*.

About 3 weeks ago, my pimple-faced wife ran out of blood pressure medicine and we went down to K-mart and had her prescription refilled. She took 2 pills as soon as we returned home. Imagine my surprise when she died 2 hours later. It seems that she had been given pimple medication rather than blood pressure medicine. Fortunately, my pharmacist and I saw the funny side because her face cleared up during her stay at the morgue and we both agreed she was the prettiest dead person we had ever seen.

Last year I took my son camping in South Florida. Imagine my surprise when a big ol' 14-foot gator attacked my son and bit his head off. I dreaded the trip home. I figured my wife would be a wee bit irritated. After all, he was our only child. Fortunately for me, she saw the funny side when I presented her with a beautiful pair of alligator shoes and matching purse. She was the talk of the funeral.

THE $129.20 FAMILY VACATION

Well, the Bull finally broke down and agreed to take his three yard apes, Marly, Brandy and Danielle, on a week long vacation to South Florida. What the heck, I had saved up $129.20 over the past year and it was burning a hole in my K-mart jeans pocket. We slept in the Toyota and I pre-made 535 tuna sandwiches so we had our room and board covered. Just remember, we had only $129.20.

HERE'S WHAT WE DID

DAY ONE: I bought $100 worth of rot-gut scotch to help me put up with 3 kids for a week. That still left $29.20.

DAY TWO: We spent the entire day at **Bill's Water World**. It consisted of a garden hose and a sprinkler. The kids weren't that happy but the 30¢ (each) admission fee fit my budget just fine. Cost $1.20.

DAY THREE: My kids love my war stories about Vietnam and they've always wanted to see some "live action," so I took them for a drive on I-95 in Jacksonville to get a first-hand look at snipers firing at us from the overpasses. My 13-year-old was wounded but she can't wait to get back in school and show off her scars. Cost $27,500 (but the city of Jacksonville picked up the tab).

DAY FOUR: What's a trip to Florida without a visit to Disney World? Wonderful, if you must know. Instead we went to **Bill's Theme Park**. He lets you *stand in line* for 3 hours for only 50¢ a person — a $29.50 savings over Disney. Cost $2.00.

DAY FIVE: My kids always wanted to visit a foreign country so I took them to Miami. Cost $10 ($2.50 each for the passport photos).

DAY SIX: For some reason, kids like the thrill of a hurricane. Since none was forecast, I decided to show them what it was like. We found a nice raging thunderstorm and I drove 100 mph through it with the windows rolled down. To add authenticity, after it was over I pulled into a convenience store and paid $15.00 for a one dollar bag of ice. Cost $15.00.

DAY SEVEN: Once again, it was back to see Bill (Bill is quite an entrepreneur and even wrote a book on how to vacation in Florida for 15¢ a day - it's a big hit with the homeless.) We visited **Bill's "One Flag Over Tampa."** There ain't a lot to do there but look up — but at 25¢ per person, who gives a rat's patootie?

First Read The News Article

ANN LANDERS

Wives beat up their husbands

Dear Ann: You recently published several letters taking you to task for writing about wife beaters and for totally ignoring the fact that an astonishing number of women beat up their husbands. A few days later, the en-closed article...

100%

Well, the BRD (Bull Research Dept.) was livid: Why doesn't anybody care about poor, abused men? We found 2 men who get their butts kicked on a daily basis by their female spouses.

Here are their comments:

Man #1 - "It's terrible. My wife goes out all hours of the night shopping and drinking with her friends and when she gets home she's drunk and demands sex or more money for a Midnight Madness Sale. If I refuse, she beats me into submission with her *purse*. I finally had to put 911 on redial."

Man #2 - "At first I tried to understand. My wife is a homemaker and, sure, the stress gets to her. After a hard day of letting out the cat, making the bed and watering our 3 artificial plants, she is usually in a rage by the time I get home. When I open the door it starts; she beats me viciously with her fully automatic hand-held flyswatter and then bashes the side of my head with a pillow and when it's all over, me and the kids are just left sobbing and huddled in a corner somewhere."

2 BULL Factoids
for the Price of One

Health is the slowest rate at which you can die!

A day without sunshine is like night!

WHAT'S THIS

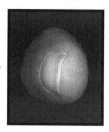

ANSWER: *Prostate's view of a doctor.*

U S A
C L O S E D
(Please call later)

☛ They laid off 800,000 non-essential workers for a week! Can you imagine? How the heck are we s'posed to run a country without our non-essential work force? There is plenty of non-essential work to be done and it's essential that it get done now!

☛ They closed the Grand Canyon! I hate it when that happens. Think of all the "Don't Feed The Bears" signs. What will the poor bears do when thousands of people can't get in to not feed them?

☛ What if another nation needed to get in touch with us. . . all they get is our national Code-A-Phone — "Thank you for calling the United States of America. We are sorry but all 800,000 of us are away from our desks til next week; however, if you would leave your nation's name, phone number and a brief statement of your position, the President will be glad to return your phone call as soon as possible. If the matter is urgent, Please press '1', if you are declaring war against us; press '2' if you would like to sign a peace treaty; press '3' and press '4' if you would like billions in foreign aid."

☛ Yes, it was terrible, closing America for an entire week. A few people probably even noticed. Okay, maybe six. Anyway, the point is, if we can get rid of 800,000 people for a week, starve a few bears and still save half a billion dollars, why not close once a month? Heck, we'd have the entire freakin' federal deficit paid off in exactly 3 years, 4 hours and 15 minutes.

Ask Granny Bull
(A sporadic column for our antique readers)

Dear Granny,
People take one look at me and think I'm as old as dirt. How old is dirt anyway?

Reader #10

Dear #10,
Dirt is 9,443,641,816,061,883,019 years old. In fact, dirt's next birthday in on January 19, 1998. Yes, dirt is a Capricorn.

Dear Granny,
I went to the doctor yesterday and he said I had only 3 years to live. In a depressing situation like this, do you have any advice to cheer me up?

Mary J.

Dear Mary,
So you're history on or about 3/1/00, huh? I've got an idea. Have that number tattooed on your forehead and go to a costume party as an expiration date.

Dear Granny,
I am 50 years old and I would like my grave marker to say I lived to be exactly 100 years old. What should I do?

Al S.

Dear Al,
Die now and multiply by 2.

Dear Granny,
I was just diagnosed with terminal mumps. You once said there was one great thing about mumps. Please tell me, what is it?

Kay K.

Dear Kay,
That *you* have them and *I* don't.

WHAT'S THIS?

THANKS FOR SHOPPING AT PIGGLY WIGGLY

ANSWER: *Alabama Samsonite*

NEWSTIME

THIS JUST IN —Poland announced today that it will no longer fly its flag at half-mast during times of national mourning. They say that removing the bottom half of all those flag poles is just too expensive.

◄ ....

Bull QUESTION TIME

Q: What has four legs and a bloody arm?
A: A happy pit bull.

......................................►

F. LEE BAILEY DECLARED
T E R M I N A L

Doctors announced today that famous trial lawyer F. Lee Bailey has 48 hours to live. Bailey went straight home and began looking for loop holes in the Bible.

HOW TO COOK A
TURKEY
(A holiday cooking tip from Thuh Bull)

Step 1: Go buy a turkey
Step 2: Take a drink of whiskey (Scotch)
Step 3: Put turkey in the oven
Step 4: Take another 2 drinks of whiskey
Step 5: Set the degree at 375 ovens
Step 6: Take 3 more whiskeys of drink,
Step 7: Turn the oven on
Step 8: Take 4 whisks of drinky
Step 9: Turk the bastey
Step 10: Whiskey another bottle of get
Step 11: Stick a turkey in the thermometer
Step 12: Glass yourself a pour of whiskey
Step 13: Bake the whiskey for 4 hours
Step 14: Pour another whisk of glasskey
Step 15: Take the oven out of the turkey
Step 16: Floor the turkey up off of the pick
Step 17: Turk the carvey
Step 18: Get yourself another scottle of Botch
Step 19: Tet the sable and pour yourself a glass of turkey
Step 20: Bless the saying, pass and eat out

BULL *Soap Update. . .*

I n 1964, our reporter saw each of the following soap operas. He hasn't seen them since but that ain't a problem. If you've seen it once, you've seen it all.

UP-TO-THE-MINUTE SOAP UPDATE

Young And The Restless: Old what's-his-face did his brother's wife and now the plot thickens. The rich guy has some problems of his own and you-know-who is about to do you-know-what to you-know-whom.

Days Of Our Lives: Suddenly an old face appears and she is the talk of the town. Several people on the show are having affairs and you-know-who is in love with you-know-who. Tune in Friday when you will hear you-know-who say you-know-what to you-know-who.

All My Children: Don't miss this week's show when our favorite soap star discovers a shocking secret about you-know-what, and what's-his-name might be to blame. And believe it or not, on Friday there will be a cliffhanger about —

well, we can't tell you and you know why.

Another World: Danger lurks for you-know-who and most of the stars will stand real close to each other so the camera will catch the look on so-and-so's face when he is finally told the truth. And you-know-who is pregnant but the father is not what's-his-face.

As The World Turns: You-know-who will be caught kissing old what's-his-face and tempers will flare. A surprise is in store for so-and-so and only the viewers and the cast and the directors and the rest of civilization know who.

Guiding Light: A confrontation will take place between you-know-who and what's-her-face. New light will be shed on an old affair between whatchamacallit and the jerk and several people will have their lives torn apart by so-and-so.

NOTICE: *And there you have it, a complete update. If you happen to go into a coma tomorrow and sleep for 35 years, don't forget to read this again when you wake up and you won't have missed a thing.*

WHAT'S THIS?

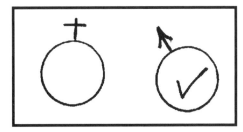

ANSWER: *The check's in the male.*

NOTICE ©

This book is close captioned for the hearing impaired.

A Morning In The Life Of A Lawyer

6:30 a.m.: Wake up and fix yourself a nice cup of piping hot venom.

6:35 a.m.: Accidentally pocket your kid's lunch money.

6:37 a.m.: Think about 10 of your richest clients for 20 seconds, round it off to the next nearest hour and bill them for it.

6:42 a.m.: Get dressed all by yourself and go to work.

6:50 a.m.: If possible, follow an ambulance.

6:51 a.m.: Stop at an accident scene. While everybody else is administering first aid, you're administering business cards.

7:00 a.m.: Write a legal contract that has 13,351 whereases, heretofores and a few 60 letter words in it. Make sure all the words in the contract are at least one-millionth of an inch high so they can easily be read using nothing at all but a Hubbell telescope.

8:15 a.m.: Read the obituaries and send all the families concerned your nice little "how a wrongful death can mean hundreds of thousands of dollars in cash and prizes" letter.

9:00 a.m.: Fire your secretary for even suggesting you return a phone call.

9:15 a.m.: Give one of your famous, free 5-word initial consultations. . . "My retainer fee is $5,000."

9:16 a.m.: Give another one.

9:17 a.m.: And another one.

9:45 a.m.: Settle out of court for $300,000 because your client sued, at your advice, over work related hiccups. Explain to your client that after all fees and costs, he gets nothing and actually owes you money, but because of your kindheartedness, you'll be glad to finance it for him at only 23% interest, compounded semi-secondly.

10:23 a.m.: The Yellow Pages representative calls and wants to know if your new personal injury ad is ready. You tell her 'yes'(**see it on next page**). ──────────▶

11:58 a.m.: Suddenly your secretary comes screaming into your office saying that your wife is on the phone. It's an emergency, your 5-year-old child has just drowned! You tell your secretary, "Ask her if it was in our pool or the neighbor's. If it was our pool, tell her I'm busy."

A real life *Yellow Pages* ad

A STUBBED TOE TO YOU . . . could be a personal injury lawsuit to us!

True Story

I was walking down the paper goods aisle at Albertsons when all of a sudden a display of paper cups came crashing down on me. Imagine being trapped under 4 ounces of rubble for almost three seconds. Now I know how those folks in Oklahoma must have felt. I was so upset I could barely keep shopping for 8 more hours! I thought my life was in total ruin. Then I remembered a billboard that said, "Sue now, ask questions later." I picked up the phone and called the law firm of Ambulance Catchers, Inc. (that's right, they not only chase ambulances, they catch them!) I'm glad I did. We settled out of court for $650,000 in cash/prizes. I am writing this testimonial from my new island home in the South Pacific. I need to add a pool though, so I'm going shopping at Sears tomorrow.

OUR SPECIALTIES

☞ Paper cuts
☞ Rug burns
☞ Stubbed toes
☞ Hot coffee spills
☞ Accidental bumps
☞ Scratches
☞ Parking lot dings
☞ Cold coffee spills
☞ Slipping down near "Watch Your Step" signs
☞ Wrongful dog barking
☞ And many other insignificant accidents

AMBULANCE CATCHERS, INC.
"We help you get what's coming to us."
875-SUED

COMPARATIVE ANATOMY:
B R A I N S

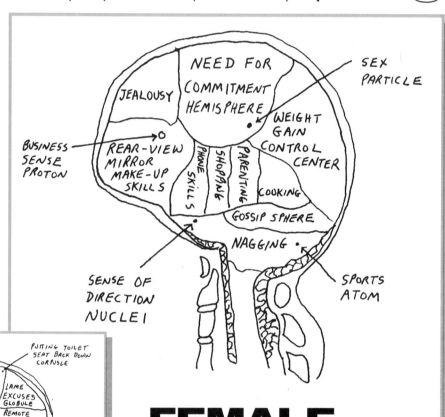

FEMALE

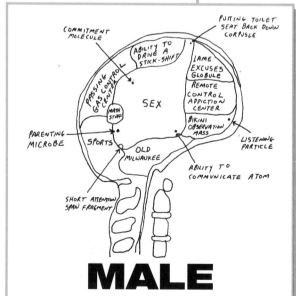

MALE

Publisher Admits To MANIPULATING HUMOR In BULL Publication

Washington, D.C. — After nearly 6 years of investigation, Congress has indicted members of the Bull writing staff for purposely extracting and adding humor to its publication, thus causing 11 . . . maybe even 12 readers to become addicted.

Other Charges . . . etc.

☞ Humor causes cancer, but to be fair, it was found that at Bull laboratories instead of using rats, Bull scientists performed experiments only on little, tiny white lawyers.

☞ From now on, all jokes must be accompanied by a Surgeon General's warning. For instance:

> **Surgeon General's Warning:**
> Farmer's daughter jokes may cause dizziness, throat cancer, low birth weight and possibly even, in more severe cases, laughter.

☞ The publisher has admitted to encouraging readers to read more than one pack of jokes per day.

☞ Restaurants and other public facilities must immediately provide patrons with "No-Joking" sections.

☞ McDonald's has jumped on the band wagon and will be the first national chain to offer a completely "Joke Free Environment". . . which by the way, should compliment their "Taste Free Food" nicely.

MOM WRITES SON

Dear Son,

Your parole officer was right, it's a lot cheaper to put you through 20 years of prison rather than 4 years of college.

Your Grand Dad was in a terrible wreck last week. He's 97 you know. Fortunately, they were able to get him out with the Gums of Life.

Speaking of accidents, your brother John was exposed to nuclear radiation last week. Fortunately it's not as bad as it sounds. We might bury him later, but right now our generator is out so we're just using him to power the farm.

Hang on a minute, someone's at the door. . . I'm back, it was just someone dressed up as a cookie trying to sell little Girl Scout dolls. I bet it was your Paw, he's such a prankster. In fact, on April Fool's Day, he burnt down our church. What a silly character he is.

Oh, by the way, if you want to call, we have a new phone number. I don't know what all the numbers are, but the total is 74.

Well, gotta go.

Love Mom

P.S. If the guards don't let you see this letter, just call me Monday at 5 p.m. and I'll read it to you.

Redneck Glossary

ROOSTER: Corn-fed alarm clock

ALUMINUM FOIL: TV antenna repair kit

AT: The word you're supposed to end every sentence with (except this one).

THUMB: What works when your jumper cables don't

THE BULL SAYS:

"Don't pay full retail for jokes." Read them straight from the manufacturer . . . the Bull. Read jokes that would normally cost up to 3, maybe 4 cents each but for you, today and today only, the jokes in this book can be laughed at for less than 1 cent per joke. Offer void for the humor-impaired.

WHAT'S THIS?

ANSWER: *Chinese U-Haul*

Dear Bull,
You said you're mad because the SAT tests in college are going computerized. So, what's the problem?

Terry E.

Dear Terry,
Because my daughter got a reminder in the mail about her SAT test. It said, "Don't forget to bring a number 2 mouse."

THIS JUST IN FROM ENGLAND

Friends say Princess Di really wanted to be Queen. Unfortunately for her, it looks like she'll have to leave that job to Elton John.

NEWSTIME

THIS JUST IN —Technology has finally caught up with baby names. For $29.95 you can buy a computer program that will give you 450,000 names to choose from. In fact, a Polish couple in New York used the program last week to name their two new twins. . . *'Click Here'* and *'Cancel.'*

DON'T
READ THIS BOOK
IF THE 'SEAL' IS TORN!

THOSE SUCKING "GARAGE" SALES

I've often written about the low-lifes that get up every Saturday morning, take off their make-up, put their hair in curlers and head to the nearest garage sale. Well, first let me explain to you that they always mis-spell it. . . it ain't GARAGE it's GARBAGE, as in garbage sales. The below list is true; people were actually trying to sell the trash listed below last Saturday morning.

Actual List

✓ 7 feet of a 25-foot extension cord... 35¢
✓ A broken blue thing...............10¢
✓ A Box of already used (and signed) Christmas cards... 25¢
✓ 2.5 percent of a matching set of hubcaps..............$1.00
✓ A stain with a dress attached to it.....................$2.00
✓ A Scrabble game with everything intact except the contents. .35¢
✓ A lava lamp (which, by the way, was voted as last year's "Alabama's Comeback Appliance Of The Year")... $2.00
✓ Exactly half of a pair of green socks... 5¢
✓ A nice, decorative, small vase (formerly an Old Spice bottle)...10¢
✓ A Polaroid snapshot of someone's niece.... 5¢

And Finally

✓ A rake that wouldn't..... 20¢

SHOWROOM CONDITION
ONLY 15,301 ORIGINAL FEET

As we all know, used car lots in the South hold the Guiness Book world record for false advertising. Up North, Chambers of Commerce are the false advertising champions with tourist-grabbing slogans like . . . "Visit New Jersey, We'll Make You Feel More At Home Than The Fetal Position."

The above slogan, of course, inspired our own Southern car lots to counter with . . . "One Owner, Little Old Lady and Church Story, Only 15,301 Original Feet (Not miles, feet) On It."

As a matter of fact, the false advertising title is no longer up for grabs. Southern car lots and Yankee Chambers of Commerce are co-champions for life.

So who's number two? Well, I don't know about up North, but down South, the 2nd Place spot is being hotly contested between restaurants and furniture stores. Today we'll take a look at restaurants.

I honest to God believe all restaurant owners are second string used car salesmen. Slogans like "Homemade Pies" and "Just Like Your Granny Used To Cook" pretty well prove it.

Recently I was in Enterprise, Alabama, attending a class reunion. While there I went into a restaurant that advertised "Southern Cooking" and "Homemade Pies." The owner's name was Rajeed Muhammad so naturally I assumed they were referring to *southern* India. I let that one pass, but I asked the waitress who's home they used to bake the "homemade pies." She glared at me and then snapped, "you ain't from around here, are you, boy?" She then turned and marched off. Needless to say, I left pieless.

Before I go on, I better head off some mail by defining "pieless." It is an adjective that means "without pie." I'll admit, before I used the word, I looked it up in the dictionary and it wasn't there. That made me nervous so I looked up the most Southern word I knew — *collard greens*.

The Webster's New Universal Unabridged and About Nine and a Half Pound Dictionary said this about collard greens. First of all, it said they aren't collard greens, they are just "collards" and it means — and I quote — "a kind of kale whose coarse leaves are borne in tufts."

To double check myself and protect my journalistic integrity, I looked up another Southern word — blackeyed peas. The dictionary defined them as — and I quote again — "the seeds of a cowpea."

By this time, I figured that the dictionary I was using must be broken, so I looked in the front and sure enough, it was published in New York.

Where was I before the preceding free English (*Southern* English) lesson? Oh yeah, a lot of restaurants claim their food is "just like your Granny used to cook."

Well, I went into one such restaurant yesterday and asked the chef, "Excuse me, sir, how did my granny season her kale whose coarse leaves are borne in tufts?" He said, "Say what?" I said, "Never mind, how long did my granny cook her delicious seeds of a cowpea?" While he was escorting me out the door he was asking, "Where you from, boy, and who the heck is your granny?!"

As always, your presence in this article has made it a truly festive occasion.

SHE'S SHE'S HOT FREE
and We Called

"Murder She Wrote" will finally end because everybody in Cabot Cove will be dead.

So we here at the Bull decided to call her. Here is part of the actual conversation.

Her: "Helloo, this is Mona. If you don't mind, I just stepped out of the shower and I can't find a towel anywhere. . . ."
(We wondered if she might be lying but we went ahead — we here at the Bull spare no expense on an investigation, even if it's costing us 30 cents a minute.)
Bull: "Mona, what can we talk about?"
Mona: "I'm glad you asked that (she was talking in a deep, sexy voice). I want it, I want it bad, tell me you've got it, tell me you can satisfy my every need, please, I beg of you, I haven't had one all day and I want a hard one, oh yes! a 3-inch hard one and I'll make your wildest dreams come true."
Bull: "A 3-inch hard what?"
Mona: "A credit card, you idiot. I need your credit card number now, oh please, give it to me now."
Bull: "First, tell me what you look like."
Mona: "I'm a 22-year-old blue-eyed blonde, 115 pounds and built like a shick brit house."
Bull: "Mona, I'm with the Bull investigative department. Tell me what you **really** look like and I'll send you a check for $100 made out to you personally at your home address."
Mona: "Okay, it's true. If you took Roseanne in one hand and Newt Gingrich in the other and smashed them together, you'd have me."
Bull: CLICK.

BULL Factoid

It's a lot easier for five women to keep a secret if four of them are dead.

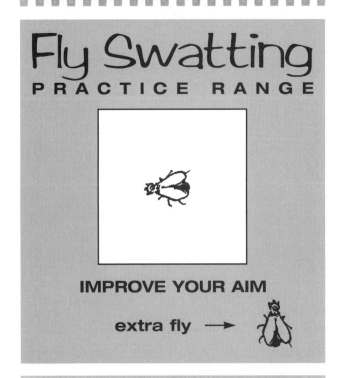

Fly Swatting
PRACTICE RANGE

IMPROVE YOUR AIM

extra fly ➔

BULL INSULT #004

by Jim S.

"You are a fine example of why some species eat their young."

BULL'S RULES:
How To Raise A Teenager

As we all know, there are only 2 choices when raising a teenager - (A) Don't, (B) Put it up for adoption. Personally, I prefer choice A. Whenever one of my kids turns 13, I freeze it and thaw it out when it reaches 21 years of age. I used to put them up for adoption but the new parents wouldn't even get out of the driveway before bringing them back, all P.O.'d and saying something about false advertising.

If you must raise a teenager

1. First, let us pray, "May God have mercy on your soul."
2. To help you afford to raise it, sell everything you own and buy stock in MTV and Clearasil futures.
3. Buy yourself an industrial strength electric cattle prod.
4. Immediately join the T.P.S.G. (Teenage Parent Support Group). Memberships are only $75,000 a year and well worth it.
5. Find out if you lucked up and got a good teenager. Ask it to do a simple chore like, for instance, dusting the top of a thimble. The odds of it doing the chore are much higher than you might think . . . almost 1 in 352 million will do exactly what they are told.
6. Buy a disposable bedroom — don't ask me why, just do it!
7. If it wants to invite all its friends over for a spend-the-night party, just rent a football stadium. It not only saves wear and tear on the house, but your community probably needed a new football stadium anyway.
8. Never, ever buy your kid a cheap pair of $60 tennis shoes from K-mart; somebody could get hurt. I tried it and my 15-year-old filed child abuse charges against me in Federal Court . . . and won! Besides, Nike and Reebok aren't as expensive as you think. I got her a pair of Reeboks last week for only $100 down and $37.50 a month for 5 years.
9. If you have a female teenager, I would highly recommend a sex change. If not, you might as well plan on having her monthly make-up bill included in your mortgage payment.
10. And finally, when the day comes that it finally turns 16 and is ready for the joy and thrill of driving, you have but one option and that, as we all know, is a good old-fashioned suicide attempt.

More HeartWarming

Letters to **THUH BULL**

My sweetheart and I recently went to Lover's Leap to commit suicide. Imagine my sweetie's surprise as I took a deep breath, counted to three and yelled, "Jump!" and didn't. She did. Fortunately for me, I saw the funny side because I had the keys to her new Mercedes 350SL in my pocket.

Recently, I called 911 because my husband was in full cardiac arrest. When the ambulance arrived, imagine my surprise when the medical technician said he was hungry and wouldn't work to save my husband 'til I fixed him a nice bologna sandwich, hold the mayonnaise, and a glass of milk. I happily agreed and my husband died, but fortunately the family and I saw the funny side because the ambulance service is giving us 10% off on their next visit of equal or lesser value.

Last night I had to work late and when I finished, I called my wife to see if she would join me for dinner. She said I should go on without her because she was in bed with the flu. Imagine my surprise when I decided to go straight home and found her in bed with my best friend, Flu Johnson. Fortunately we all saw the funny side. We laughed and joked about his name being "Flu" and her tricking me into thinking she was sick. Then I stabbed them to death.

I teach 11th grade at a local high school. The children are just so rude. Recently, I told my class that I was going to make an example out of the next student who was rude. The entire class immediately got up and mooned me. Imagine their surprise when I sprayed the room with automatic gunfire. Then they all sat down, except of course for the three dead students, and finished their poetry lesson. Fortunately we all saw the funny side because the 3 dead students didn't like poetry anyway.

THUH BULL

MACHO BULL Factoid

When a man talks dirty to a woman, it's sexual harassment; when a woman talks dirty to a man, it's $4.95 per minute!

Loose News

☞ A member of the Platters left the band and is going out on his own. He will call himself "The Plate."

☞ Like a miner digging for traces of silver, Dan Rather interviewed Colin Powell and finally struck an opinion.

☞ The new Betty Crocker facelift ain't all that's changing. Now General Mills is going after the Asian market with cupcakes marinated in soy sauce.

WHAT'S THIS?

•

ANSWER: *A Polish Connect-A-Dot Instructional Game (Advanced)*

ANOTHER BULL
"Wrong Word"
CONTEST

Can you spot the word (or words) that don't fit in the following paragraph? If you can't, either you're blind or stupid.

Lucy was the most gorgeous girl I had ever seen. It had been six years since I had seen her. She was back and she was ready. We met at her hotel room. She opened the door. I couldn't believe my eyes. She was stark-dressed. She pulled me close and stuck her warm, pink, boat anchor half way down my throat. We fell to the bed and made wild and passionate oatmeal cookies. Then we both smoked a turkey and fell asleep.

WHAT'S THIS?

ANSWER:

Redneck Peeping Tom
Thanks to Ed S.

FOREIGN PETS

I was drinking a few dozen beers the other night when I noticed a Russian boy on TV who was talking about his pet goldfish. Actually, it never occurred to me that goldfish were anywhere but at my cousin Vinny's house and at Kmart. We did a special report on foreign pets. We call it . . .

A SPECIAL REPORT ON FOREIGN PETS

- In Africa, we met a boy whose pets included a herd of wild elephants and about 13,000 monkeys. Just like an American mom, his mom makes them stay outside except when it rains.

- In Poland, we met a young girl who had a talking parrot. It could say "duh" in 14 foreign languages.

- In San Francisco (if that ain't a foreign country, I don't know what is) we met a happily married gay couple that had a "Beware Of Butterfly" sign in their front yard.

- In Korea, we couldn't seem to find any pet dogs. We finally found a little boy playing with his dog. We said, "My, that is a cute little dog. What do you call him?" He said, "I call him Fido but my Mom calls him 'Tomorrow's Pot Roast.'"

- We met a little girl in Saudi Arabia who was holding her cat and crying. We asked her what was wrong and she said her Mom was making her take it back to the Mid-East Humane Society. We asked why. She said, "Because I can't train him to use the desert."

Thuh Bull recently purchased Publisher's Clearing House. No changes will be made except on the envelope it will say, "You may already be a gullible loser!"

FEMALE CLASSIFIEDS

10 MISC. HELP WANTED

I am going on vacation. I need a woman to come stay at my home for 2 weeks. Duties include light cooking, nagging and maybe a little heavy-duty shopping so my husband won't miss me too much.

12 MISC. FOR SALE

Ann's Rearview Mirror Store — Opening Soon. Your makeup never had it so good. Come see the largest selection of rearview mirrors in the Southeast. Over 15,000 to choose from.

30 MISC. INSTRUCTION

Learn to Power Gossip! Are you tired of your low-level, ineffective gossiping? You know, you hear a nasty rumor and you can't even enhance it to make it more destructive? Not anymore! With Sara's School of Gossip, you can derail a friend's entire future with just 5 easy words or cause a full-scale revolt at your office with my "Office Scam Gossip Plan." Call today and ruin a life tomorrow!

40 AUTOS FOR SALE

I have a pretty blue car for sale. It has all the normal stuff on it and it gets mileage and has a big red thing on it that I don't know to use and the keys are a beautiful shade of silver. Also, if you know a mechanic, the hood will open and there's lots of things under it that are included in the price. The car is not very old either.

65 YARD SALE

13-woman Yard Sale. Starts this Saturday about eleven-ish. Items include used makeup, plenty of those exciting, hard-to-find knitting utensils, a log cabin made entirely out of tampons, and 27,00 pairs of shoes. **Directions:** Go over to that nice street near the college with all the pretty flowers on it, take either a left, or possibly a right at that lovely gray house and go down that street for a few minutes till you come to that hill and take a left. Refreshments will be served. Casual attire is permitted and we have name-tags so you can meet and mingle with all our other yard shopping guests.

THIS JUST IN

Krystal's hamburgers made it in the news this week. Last month they sold over 250,000 hamburgers. If it keeps up, they're gonna have to kill another cow.

Thanks to Ron B.

I'm the entire Krystal inventory.

SOUTH KICKS
YANKEE BUTT

Bull Headquarter, Florida — Okay, all you history butts (or is it buffs?), it's time to get one thing straight. The South won the Civil War, not the North. I found a document in my Great Grandfather Bull's cedar chest that relates just one of 312,415 examples of how the South kicked butt and took names. See document to right. (Historical note: The document was typed on the first typewriter in history — it was so old it typed in *pencil.*)

Who would be most interested in this ad?

FOR SALE

1979 JOHN DEERE RUNS GOOD BUT MISSING SEAT AND STEERING WHEEL

JOHN DEERE

ANSWER: A person who has lost his butt and doesn't know which way to turn

May 8, 1864

Dear Luke,

I only shot 67 Yankees today, but a friend of mine had better luck. Here's what happened. . . .

As General Sherman was passing Stone Mountain, on his way from Atlanta to the sea, a Rebel soldier was on top of the mountain shouting obscenities at the Yankee soldiers. General Sherman sent 50 troops up the mountain to kill the Rebel. After an hour, only one Yankee soldier returned; all the others had been killed by the Rebel. Meantime, the Rebel continued yelling obscenities. General Sherman then sent 500 troops up the mountain to kill the Rebel. Once again only one returned. The rebel soldier once again began shouting obscenities and threats. Well, by now General Sherman was getting a wee bit P.O.'d. He ordered 10,000 troops to storm the mountain. About half way up the mountain all 10,000 troops suddenly began to retreat back down the mountain screaming, "General, General, it's a trick! There's *two* of them up there!"

Good Shooting,

Capt. Bull

Making kids clean their plates is abusive

Remove the plate witho... offer no su...titutes

Dear Ann: I feel compelled to write after reading the letter from "An Aunt in Greenfield, Mass.," whose sister, Dora, ...motionally abuses her children by forcing ...everything on their plates.

SPECIAL REPORT

Evidently, while God is on a two-week vacation catching some rays in another universe, Ann Landers has appointed herself to take over (as witnessed by the above headline. . . **"Making Kids Clean Their Plate Is Abusive"**).

So what's gonna happen tonight in millions of homes all across America. . .

Mom: "Susie, please finish your mashed potatoes."

Susie: "Not gonna do it."

Mom: "Excuse me?"

Susie: "Mashed potatoes bite. Not gonna eat them."

Mom: "Okay, young lady, you can just sit right there 'til Dad gets home, no TV, no dessert, nothing."

(When Mom is in the kitchen washing dishes, Susie make a phone call)

Actual 911 Call

911 Operator: "Yes, what is your emergency?"

Susie: "Child abuse."

911 Operator: "What type of abuse, physical, sexual. . . ?"

Susie: "No, much worse. Mom insisted I join the Clean Plate Club."

911 Operator: "Are you positive?"

Susie: "Yes, I wouldn't joke about that."

911 Operator: "Okay, I want you to remain clam. Tell me, Susie, is the abuser still in the house?"

Susie: "Yes, and she's at it again."

911 Operator: "Okay Susie, we've got help on the way, 2 S.W.A.T. teams, 4 police cruisers and the National Guard. What is the abuser doing now?"

Susie: "She's threatening to kill my brother if he doesn't clean his room."

911 Operator: "Did she use the word 'kill'?"

Susie: "Not exactly. She said, 'Clean your room Jimmy or no baseball Saturday' . . . and that would kill him."

911 Operator: "What a miserable bum your Mom must be!"

Susie: "Yeah, a real bad one. Oh, I see a patrol car in the drive . . . oh no, operator, you sent the wrong unit, the car says 'Broccoli Police' not 'Mashed Potato Patrol.'"

911 Operator: "No, it's okay Susie, we're just running short handed after the Ann Landers article came out. Don't worry though, the Broccoli Police are cross-trained to handle mashed potato emergencies. Well, I gotta go, we've got a liver and onion red alert on line 3."

(Thanks, Ann — you bite!)

McDonald's has introduced the "Arch Deluxe," a quarter-pounder with peppery bacon and two kinds of mustard. A company spokesman said it was "developed in order to appeal to more sophisticated tastes" (True) . . . What we want to know is how they get away with using "McDonald's" and "sophisticated taste" in the same sentence.

Dear Bull,
    What is the number one complaint of Alabama Police?

            Signed,
            Bubba the 13th

A TWO-FOR-ONE Mother's Day promotion backfired in Henderson, N.C., after a jewelry store offered a free gun with the purchase of a diamond ring. The ads were pulled after numerous complaints from customers. (True) . . . "Evidently they were mad about the seven-day waiting period for the ring."

Dear Bubba,
    The City Council is always too quick to call in Batman.

A teacher in England just invented a new board game called "How To Make Children." One aspect involves throwing sperm and egg dice to hit a fertility square in mid-ovulation. (True) . . . "I was trying to buy the T&A Railroad when my opponent caught me shooting blanks and I had to go back three spaces."

BULL INSULT #307
I didn't say you were skinny. I just said you could rent yourself out as a ring sizer.

 *Oh No!*

FEMALE CAR SALESMEN

Oh no, just when we thought we had men and all their 837 lies it takes them to sell a used car figured out, the used car dealers are starting to use women. It ain't fair! Here are a few lies we were told yesterday by Ima Cheeter down at Easy Mike's Used Cars. (See lies below)

LIES BELOW

♥ "First, let's take a look at the most important part of any transportation system. . . the rearview mirror. It has had only 1,200 original make-up jobs done on it, and as you can tell, it is extra wide for your grooming pleasure. Plus, Easy Mike will guarantee you can do a full makeover with it at even the busiest of intersections. And today, and today only, buy the rearview mirror for only $9,995 and we'll throw in the car that is attached to it absolutely FREE!"

♥ "Over here we have a 1989 blue car. Blue, of course, is for boys and over there is a nice 1992 pink car for the little lady in your family. As you know, Consumer Reports rates blue and pink cars as the best cars in America for the past 10 years. . . What, do we have a 1986 green car? No, here at Easy Mike's we only sell cars that match my wardrobe."

♥ "Let's talk about power. Under the hood of this car is a big gear, or something like that, that is more powerful than 15 blow dryers going full blast at a beauty salon. Can you imagine?"

♥ "Look at this dashboard — a real beaut, ain't she? My favorite parts are the beautifully colored warning lights that match most shades of lipstick. And, imagine driving down the road when the nice red and yellow oil warning signal lights up just at sunset. You talk about romantic!"

♥ "And here at Easy Mike's, when you buy a car from us, you know you'll never ever have to change the oil again. That's right, when that oil warning signal comes on, get the most out of it. Sometimes it will frantically come on and off for 20, even 30 delightful miles. Then when your car finally freezes up, don't worry, Easy Mike will be glad to sell you another car for only full retail plus 25% shipping and handling."

♥ "Well, let's just go inside where I've got another surprise for you. Our credit applications are the prettiest in town. A nice shade of peach with just a hint of lilac should make even the wariest of buyers relax."

The Bull and The Used Car Salesman

Me: "The odometer looks like it's been tampered with."
UCS: "Oh no, we just had it out to service it. You never know when your odometer might go out and cause a major pile up on the interstate."

Me: "What kind of mileage does it get?"
UCS: "Incredible! Yesterday, we put a gas saving device on it and I took it out for a spin. Before I had driven 5 miles the tank overflowed."

(We took our recorder)
Me = me, UCS = Used Car Salesman

Me: "How many miles on the engine?"
UCS: "Uh,uh, seventy-eight."
Me: "You mean there are only 78 miles on this car?"
UCS: "Uh, no, the little ole lady drove it only 78 times."
Me: "Tell me the truth, where did she drive it 78 times?"
UCS: "Uh, Afghanistan. But she always parked it in a garage."

Me: "Will you finance it for me and what are the terms?"
UCS: "Of course. All we need is your first born, $14,995 down and we'll finance the balance all the way 'til next weekend."
Me: "To tell the truth, I'm with the Bull. I'm here to do a story on used car salesmen."
UCS: "Oh, heck! I reckon now is as good a time as any to quit and become a TV evangelist."

Thought For The Day **"Never go to sleep mad. . . stay up and fight!"**

THE GREAT AMERICAN
BACKYARD BARBECUE

4:15 p.m.: Go to store, buy $3 worth of chicken and $6 worth of charcoal, (remember last time).

4:18 p.m.: Get home.

4:20 p.m.: Go back to the store, buy $3 worth of charcoal lighter. No, make that $30 worth, (remember last time).

4:26 p.m.: Go by gas station. Get $2 worth of Amoco unleaded in case charcoal won't light.

4:40 p.m.: Get home.

4:41 p.m.: Go back to store. Buy one of every conceivable thing you can cook on a grill. The Smith kid hates chicken, not to mention everything else.

4:58 p.m.: The first guests arrive.

5:01 p.m.: Go back to store and buy the beer you assumed the guests would bring.

5:20 p.m.: Get home, light charcoal. Cover grill so guests won't see how rusty it is.

5:30 p.m.: Guest tells you charcoal went out. Also tells you how rusty the grill is.

5:31 p.m.: Relight charcoal. Listen to guest ask you why you would want to ruin perfectly good food by cooking it on the grill in the first place.

5:33 p.m.: More guests arrive.

5:38 p.m.: Go to store because these guests drink only Coke. Consider not going back home. Wonder how much a one way Delta flight is to anywhere.

5:50 p.m.: Get home with Coke. Smith kid tells you he drinks only Pepsi. Call Delta, they're only $375. Naw, might P.O. the wife.

5:53 p.m.: Guests milling around backyard. Neighbor's Great Dane starts to bark incessantly. Consider a shot to his head with your deer rifle. Naw, it might P.O. the neighbor.

5:55 p.m.: Ask everyone how they like their chicken cooked. Get only 2 answers that are the same, which isn't really that bad considering you've got only 37 guests.

5:59 p.m.: When no one is looking, throw about half a gallon of unleaded on to jump-start the fire.

6:00 p.m.: Throw the chicken and other crap on the grill and go get yourself a cold beer, which, of course, you're out of.

6:10 p.m.: The neighbor calls and complains that your guests are making his dog bark. You could have sworn it was supposed to be the other way around. You wish you'd bought that silencer for your deer rifle.

6:14 p.m.: The guests start offering free grilling tips like: "You should have started the charcoal 4 hours ago," and "You should never put barbecue sauce on 'til 7 minutes before it's done."

6:20 p.m.: Take chicken legs off the grill. Listen as guests say sarcastically, "Oh, just the way I like them, burnt on the outside, yet frozen solid near the bone."

6:28 p.m.: Naturally, a thunderstorm decides to stop directly over your backyard. All the guests crowd into your living room.

6:30 p.m.: Someone yells that the grill's on fire — all the food is burning. You send the Smith kid out supposedly to check the grill, but if the truth must be known, you're hoping he'll be struck by lightning.

6:31 p.m.: A bolt of lightning strikes. You look outside. There's good news and bad news. The bad news is, it missed the Smith kid . . . the good news, the neighbor's dog is now just a furry pile of smoldering wreckage, kinda like the food on your grill.

6:33 p.m.: You excuse yourself to go order a pizza for everybody. You mistakenly dial the wrong number because the phone is answered by a sweet young lady who says, "Delta reservations, how may I help you?

6:45 p.m.: Once again you excuse yourself by explaining to your guests you need to run down to the store for a pack of smokes. The Smith kid wonders why you need 3 suitcases to buy cigarettes. . . .

BULL'S
Helpful Things for
WRITING LETTERS

1. Don't ever use no double negatives.
2. *Don't use commas, which ain't necessary.*
3. About those sentence fragments . . .
4. *It is important to use your apostrophe's correctly.*
5. Always proofread your writing to see if you any words out.
6. *Rember correct speling is essential.*
7. Avoid cliches like the plague.
8. *When righting, remember, sum words sound alike, butt aren't.*
9. Don't write run-on sentences they are hard to read people can't understand them.
10. *If you are dyslexic, always remember to put a sentence at the end of your period.*
11. Never write a preposition at the end of a sentence because people can see where it's at.
12. *Ain't ain't a word.*
13. Don't mke maek make sloppy lk look looking coar corrections.

You want flies with that?

Women In Combat

Calvin Klein agrees to manufacture a beautiful, bullet proof combat purse

As our policy states, we here at the Bull offer equal opportunity discrimination. It was recently pointed out to us that we haven't bashed women lately, for which we apologize. We sent our team of 1 reporter to study women in combat. Below is our report.

OUR REPORT

★ On a recent battlefield in Sarajevo, a female Army lieutenant was overheard saying, "Will you just look at what the enemy is wearing today? They ought to be ashamed of themselves!"

★ During the Bosnia invasion, Capt. Lucy Smith was driving her tank to work when she realized it had no rearview mirror. "My God," she was heard screaming at her commander, "what if I were killed wearing no make-up? If people saw me like this I would just die!" (Ed note: a team of Max Factor emergency make-up personnel was quickly flown in to remedy Capt. Smith's situation.)

★ An amendment to the Geneva Convention (where all nations agree to use their war manners when fighting each other) is being considered. The proposed amendment states: During hand-to-hand combat between two females of opposing countries, each combatant will have 2 time-outs per battle. Even if one female has a decided advantage and is about to blow the other's head off, she can

still call a 5-minute time-out to "fix her hair and freshen up a bit."

★ A rather creative female Navy pilot recently was in a dog-fight with an Iraqi jet over the no-fly zone near Kuwait the other day. The Iraqi pilot happened to be a female also. All of a sudden, the female Navy pilot radioed the Iraqi pilot, "Have I ever shown you pictures of my kids?" The Iraqi pilot said, "No, but I would love to see them." And she flew her jet right next to the Navy girl, who promptly unleashed a heat-seeking missile up the Iraqi lady's kazoo. She was later awarded the Peach Heart for valor. (Women hate purple.)

WHAT'S THIS?

ANSWER: *The top view of Nixon's casket.*

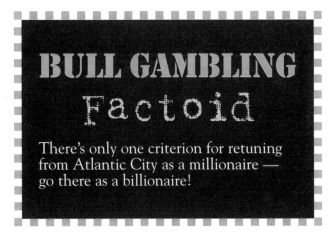
Bull History Lesson

If you don't know how Hitler took Poland so easily in WWII, I'll tell you. He marched in backwards and told them he was *leaving*.

Unclassified Ad

Polyester support groups forming now. If you, or anyone you know, are still hooked on leisure suits, act now . . . or it may be too late.

NOTICE:

This book of BULL was written without the assistance of any sobriety whatsoever.

BULL THOUGHT

Last year 5 million kids went to summer camp. The obvious question is this . . . Is a handmade wallet really worth six hundred bucks?

How Bad Was It?

My wife's cooking is so bad that the flies all pitched in and bought her a new screen door!

2 Question Sexual Harassment Test

A lot of people are confused. What constitutes sexual harassment? Well, we here at the Bull have designed a simple little multiple choice test to help you learn the do's and don'ts. Please only answer one question at a time. You may begin.

How To Avoid It Test

1. You are sitting at your desk, minding your own business, when the most gorgeous blonde in the entire free world walks up to you, and leans over your desk, exposing what seems like 3.5 miles of the most beautiful cleavage you have ever seen.

You would:

A. Stare for 15 minutes and then run out and buy her an engagement ring.

B. Tell her a twelve hour story as a delaying tactic.

C. Grab the nearest ice-pick and stab your eyes out.

Correct answer: C

2. You and your buddies are standing by the office copier when Candy (a 10 by any man's standards) walks by wearing the shortest mini-skirt you've ever seen. Just then she drops a paper clip and bends over to pick it up.

You would:

A. Call the office supply place and immediately order an additional 15 thousand cases of paper clips and then tastefully scatter them around the office floor.

B. When she finishes picking it up, lead your fellow co-workers in a nice round of applause.

C. Quickly dive for the paper clip and hand it to her before she bends over, knowing full well that you are fixing to suffer a severe South Alabama butt whippin' from your co-workers as soon as she leaves.

Correct answer: C

BULL THOUGHT FOR THE DAY

They ought to give the electric chair to anyone convicted of terrorism. If the family wants to commemorate his passing, they can place a nice wreath on the fuse box.

Question TIME

Q. What's worse than being married to Lorena Bobbit?

A. Being divorced from O.J. Simpson.

THE MAYTAG REPAIRMAN

Overheard

(Phone ringing . . .)

Maytag Man: "Hello, you've reached the Maytag Repairman, can I help you?"

Customer: "Yes, my washing machine is flooding."

Maytag Man: "Right lady! Ain't you seen the commercials?"

Customer: "Look buster, there's 3 feet of water in my utility room and my 2-month-old son just drowned."

Maytag Man: "So I suppose your first call was to 911?"

Customer: "Yes, but they didn't know a thing about washing machines."

Maytag Man: "Yeah, and I don't know a thing about CPR so leave my butt alone. Besides that, I'm busy."

Customer: "Busy?! I've seen the commercials, jerk wad, you ain't never busy!"

Maytag Man: "I SAID. . . I'm busy."

Customer: "Doing what?"
Maytag Man: "We're shooting another TV commercial about how busy I'm not."

(Click)

NEW BULL T-SHIRT

SAVE THE WHALES
—
COLLECT THE ENTIRE SET

WHAT'S THIS?

1, 2, Earnhardt, 4, 5

ANSWER: *How a redneck counts to five.*

Dear Vet Bull,

I own an eight-year-old spider named Creepy. She is a good spider except for the time she bit and killed my sister. By the way, my spider is a Negro, and her husband was eaten by a moth years ago. Yes, she is a black widow. Anyway, she is losing her hearing. Should I get her a hearing aid or just step on her?

Jeff L.

Dear Jeff,

BELTONE just introduced a line of designer hearing aids for spiders. It's called "A Line of Designer Hearing Aids For Spiders." They are very expensive so I would just step on her.

Dear Vet Bull,

I have a nice green frog named Leap. He likes to play and eat nasty little delicious bugs, but I can't teach him to croak. Any suggestions?

Sue S.

Dear Sue,

Yes, there are several ways to make a frog croak. Personally, I prefer dropping a 75 lb. boat anchor on them.

Dear Vet Bull,

I am a cockroach lover and have been for years. I can't stand it when one dies. It breaks my heart, especially during the funeral services when I gently lay it to rest in the kitchen light fixture. What can I do to prolong the lives of my little friends?

Toni M.

Dear Toni,

We had the same problem at my house so I hired Orkin Pest Control to spray once a month. Now, all the wildlife in my house seems to be doing just fine.

WANTED
GANG MEMBER

Salary: $10,000 - Job: Not to Kill

Congratulations to the rocket scientists of Ft. Worth for figuring out how to solve the crime problem. Imagine . . .

Leroy: "Well, it's a beautiful day, the flowers are blooming, the birds are singing, I think I'll kill some one today."

Hulk: "No, don't do it."

Leroy: "Hey, man, you killed 4 people yesterday and now you are telling me not to waste a dude?"

Hulk: "Yeah, well, that was before I got hired by the city of Ft. Worth not to kill folks."

Leroy: "What's in it for me?"

Hulk: "I'll give you one thousand dollars not to kill the dude."

Leroy: "Okay, hand it over."

Hulk: "Here, but remember, you can't kill the dude for a year while I'm a city-employed gang member."

Leroy: "Not a problem, I'll just wait and kill him after your year is up."

Hulk: "No problem, so what you gonna do with the thousand?"

Leroy: "Go buy an assault weapon and kill me some dudes."

Hulk: "What! you just promised you wouldn't kill the dude!"

Leroy: "No, I ain't gonna kill *that* dude, I'm gonna kill some dudes you didn't pay me not to kill."

Hulk: "How many dudes you planning to kill?"

Leroy: "I don't know, maybe 8 or 9."

Hulk: "Man, if I pay you a thousand for every dude you don't kill, I ain't making a dime."

Leroy: "Hey man, ask the mayor for a raise. Not killing people is expensive."

Hulk: "What if he won't give me a raise?"

Leroy: "Kill the dude!"

Hulk: "Makes sense to me!"

(Footnote: Nobody was killed in Ft. Worth for an entire year at a cost of only $943,861,896,221,863,374,095.35 but chaos broke out on the 366th day and everybody in the entire city was killed. Have a nice day.)

BULL GETS "THE" INTERVIEW

Panama City Beach, Fl. — As you may have heard, O.J. Simpson visited the International Headquarters of Thuh Bull on Panama City Beach, Florida, after being found not guilty. He agreed to a 20-minute, no-holds-barred interview on one condition, that we not make up any ridiculous questions and bogus answers . . . just print the actual interview. We agreed:

Bull: "Let's start from the beginning: Did you kill Nicole Brown Simpson and Ron Goldman?"

O.J.: "Well, to be honest, yes, at first I thought I did but Johnny Cochran is so good that by the time the trial was about over he had me convinced I did not, would not, could not have committed that crime."

Bull: "Where were you during the murders?"

O.J.: "I was at Denny's waiting to get served."

Bull: "Okay, I'll buy that, but why did you have a fake beard, $10,000 in cash and a suitcase full of clothes during your one-and-a-half-hour Bronco commercial after the murders? Were you planning to escape?"

O.J.: "No, silly, I was on my way to a $10,000 per plate costume party in Cozumel."

Bull: "If you could point to one thing that proves beyond a shadow of a doubt that there is absolutely no way you could have committed those murders, what would it be?"

O.J.: "That Mark Fuhrman is a racist."

Bull: "What does that have to do with anything?"

O.J.: "Darned if I know, but the jury sure bought it."

Bull: "You tried on the bloody glove and it didn't appear to fit. What do you think that said to the jury?"

O.J.: "I don't know about them, but to me it said that 15 years of acting experience finally paid off."

Bull: "I understand you and Paula plan on marriage. What advice did your mother give you about the wedding ceremony?"

O.J.: "Mom keeps reminding me . . . *'Remember, O.J., it's kiss the bride and cut the cake, kiss the bride and cut the cake.'*"

Bull: "Why did the Dream Team keep bringing up the 'N' word?"

O.J.: "It wasn't the Dream Team, you idiot, it was the prosecution that kept bringing up the word 'knife'."

Bull: "O.J., I understand you played golf with a friend of mine, Joe."

O.J.: "Yeah, Joe's a real cut-up."

Bull: "That's funny, he said the same thing about you. Anyway, he told me you sold him your new golf video. What's the name of it?"

O.J.: "Two Slices And A Long Drive."

Bull: "Speaking of selling things to raise money, I understand for Halloween this year that they were selling O.J. Trial Halloween costumes, you know, Ito masks, Kato wigs and O.J. Black Shadowy Figure costumes. How did they sell?"

O.J.: "They sold great but almost all the kids that bought O.J. costumes returned them and demanded a refund."

Bull: "Why is that?"

O.J.: Oh, I don't know, something about the little pinheads saying the gloves didn't fit."

Bull: "Well, our 20 minutes are almost up. Before we go, I understand you said you will spend the rest of your life, if it takes it, to track down the real killer."

O.J.: "That's right."

Bull: "Well, I have a great idea where you should look first."

O.J.: "Great, where's that?"

Bull: "In a freaking mirror."

EXTRA!!! BULL EXTRA!!!

In Our Next Issue

- New bestseller, "As I Lay Dieting," big hit with local fat women
- Read how 100 men down off the coast of San Francisco and came back up as 50 couples
- Thuh Bull catches National Enquirer in a "truth"

BRAIN DEAD TRIVIA

1. What succeeds best?
2. What's brown and stands on the corner selling dead chickens?
3. What is the capital of New Jersey?

ANSWERS

1. A canary with no teeth
2. Colonel Sanchez
3. About $1.75

IRAQ'S ONLY MISTAKE

The Pentagon recently revealed that the reason Iraq's army was so soundly defeated was because they used a Russian defensive tactic:

"ENGAGE THE ENEMY"

4 RULES FOR ALL SOLDIERS

1. Never forget your weapon was made by the lowest bidder.
2. The only thing more accurate than incoming enemy fire is incoming friendly fire.
3. All "five second" grenade fuses will burn down in three seconds.
4. When you have secured an area, don't forget to tell the enemy.

Question TIME

Q. What's this? 10, 9, 8, 7, 6, 5, 4, 3, 2, 1
A. Bo Derek getting old.

Ask Dr. Bull

Dear Dr. Bull,

Is there anyway to get rid of freckles? If not, how can I make the most of them?

"Red"

Dear "Red",

No, I'm afraid there is no cure. However, you can always use them to meet new friends. Just walk up to a stranger and hand him a ballpoint pen and say, "Hi, I'm Red, wanna use my face for a quick game of connect-the-dots?"

Dear Dr. Bull,

I've often heard you use the phrase. . . "green thumb." You're so full of bull! I bet you can't even name one person that ever had a green thumb.

Dow Ting Thomas

Dear Dow,

You lose. Evidently you've never met the Jolly Green Giant's proctologist.

Dear Dr. Bull,

You used to hate chiropractors, now you love them. Why?

Dr. Smith

Dear Dr. Smith,

No, my good man, I still can't stand them but I've learned to get rich off these quacks. Every time a new one opens an office somewhere, I just rush down to my stockbroker and buy *wheelchair futures.*

Dear Dr. Bull,

With all the malpractice lawsuits going around, I bet you have to work twice as much as you used to just to afford the insurance.

Susan B.

Dear Susan,

No, actually I work less. I spend only 2 days a week working at my practice. The other 3 days I'm in court working on my defense.

Dear Dr. Bull,

I know how you hate criminals. If a bank robber is shot in the heart and brought to your office for emergency treatment, would you give him the same care you would give others?

Charles I.

Dear Charles,

Absolutely! I'd tell him to take a number and browse over our nice selection of 1978 magazines while I conclude an emergency breast exam on my new nurse.

Dear Dr. Bull,

How do you set your fees?

Pat M.

Dear Pat,

I pull a figure out of the air that you can't possibly afford and then double it.

LETTERS
TO THE JANITOR

Dear Janitor,
The letters you get under the "Dear Janitor" column are ridiculous. I bet you make up most of them. In fact, you probably made this one up.

Gary A.

Dear Janitor,
You once said that every home with children in it should never be without something to induce vomiting in case of an emergency. What product do you recommend?

Dr. H.

Dear Janitor,
Why do Polish names end with "ski"?

Dan W.

Dear Janitor,
You always turn this column into a 'sex thing' but go ahead, I give up. If, as you said, "flying is the second greatest thrill known to man," what is the first greatest thrill?

Bruce G.

Dear Gary,
No, I did. I mean, yes, I didn't.

Dear Dr. H.,
The Greatest Hits Of Barry Manilow.

Dear Dan,
I don't know, but it's probably because they can't spell "toboggan".

Dear Bruce,
Landing, you idiot.

Dear Bull,
 I saw that big rock you gave your wife for Christmas. Is it a real diamond?

Just Curious

Dear Curious,
 If it ain't, I've been cheated out of eight bucks!

TRUE
WAR STORY

Four Marines were sitting in their tent playing poker one night when their sergeant came busting through the door screaming, "About two hundred IRAQI soldiers just landed about a quarter of a mile down the beach and they're headed this way!"
 The leathernecks looked at one another wearily. Finally, one of them got up, yawned and said, "It's all right, I'm ahead, I'll go."

OVERHEARD
IN ATLANTA

BUSINESSMAN #1: "I'm sure worried that the Saudis are going to buy up all the property in America."

BUSINESSMAN #2: "Don't worry, I don't think the Japanese will sell it to them."

Thought of the Month

How can a pregnant fish tell when her water breaks?

ever WONDER ?????

You know those bags that people have under their eyes. What's in them? Maybe it's just little tiny groceries.

A Day In The Life Of A Housefly

Being a fly is very hard work. Now don't get me wrong. I had a wonderful maggothood. I was born on a dead cow and spent the first 5 weeks of my life eating its rotting liver. But then one day my wings appeared and I knew it was time to pack my things and leave cow. My instinct told me I needed to find a kitchen somewhere. My job was to P.O. family members at meal-time. I flew through a lovely neighborhood 'til I found my special welcome fly invitation — an open window. The next 5 days were the hardest of my life, not to mention the last.

Here's how the days went: At 5:30 each morning, a human would come in and make coffee and toast. I never did like toast, I'm a liver fly myself. Anyway, I would land on it and then the pinhead that lived there would roll up a copy of the Bull and swat at me. Bulls aren't good for anything, especially killing flies. After that, my job was to crash my head into windows, walk on ceilings and attack peanut butter and jelly sandwiches. At nap time, my job was to turn on my buzz switch real loud and fly real low over people. On the 5th day I flew into a window fan.

AMERICAN INGENUITY

A man in a car was riding behind a truck for a long while. He couldn't figure out why every two or three blocks the truck stopped, the driver got out, ran around the side of the truck and *slapped it* three times real hard, ran back to the wheel and drove another three blocks and repeated the incident. The man in the car couldn't stand it anymore and got out of his car and approached the truck driver. "What is your problem?" he asked the truck driver.

"You see, mister," the truck driver said, "this is a two-ton truck and I have four tons of canaries in there. I have to keep half of them flying at all times!"

ever WONDER ????

Did you ever wonder what if people had expiration dates stamped on their foreheads? You didn't? Well, I did. I wondered what Ted Kennedy's would say. Then I figured it out. It would say, "Best if drunk by 10 p.m."

OH NO YOU DON'T.
NOT WITHOUT A WASHER!

BULL Rule of Life #364

"Never trust an Oriental dentist who sells miniature ivory animals."

CAN MY MARRIAGE BE SAVED?

First, Samantha's turn.

I don't know what went wrong; we have everything in common. I'm 19, Bill is 93, I love money, he has it, and so on. Some people say they don't believe in love at first sight. I do. In fact, I fell head over heels in love with him the first time I laid eyes on his check book.

Bill just doesn't understand that a woman has needs. No, I'm not talking about in the bedroom; I'll have plenty of time for that when he's dead (which by my calculations should be sometime early next week). Right now, I'm interested in the finer things in life like staying up past 4:30 in the afternoon and not spending every Saturday morning browsing at the Wheelchair Factory Outlet.

Oh sure, he buys me pretty things. Just last month he bought me Eastern Europe, but do you realize what kind of closet space that takes up? I just don't know what to do.

Now, Bill's turn.

When I first saw Samantha, I believe it was about 3 weeks ago, I knew I had to meet her. I wheeled up to her and used my best pick-up line . . . "Hello, I'll give you three million dollars to marry me." After a lengthy 3-hour engagement, we were married later on that afternoon. (You can't mess around at my age.)

We didn't have our first argument until the vows were being exchanged. She wanted to honeymoon in Aspen and I wanted to nap in the reception hall. We got separated while they were still throwing the rice. I don't know what to do.

Now it's the analyst's turn.
Forget it.

Your 5 Basic

BLONDE JOKES

Blonde
Alabama Men are IDIOTS Too

So these two blonde D.O.T. workers were digging a ditch along I-65 in Montgomery. . . .

Worker #1: "Hey stupid, stop throwing the dirt outta the ditch."

Worker #2: "Well, I gotta put it somewhere."

Worker #1: "Well, you imbecile, dig another hole and put it there."

OVERHEARD
A G A I N

Bull: "So Blondie, how do you like your 20-room house?"
Blonde: "It's great. I furnished the living room with all the money I saved with soap coupons."
Bull: "Why didn't you furnish the other nineteen rooms?"
Blonde: "I can't do that yet. They're full of soap."

Blonde Honeymoon

They get to the hotel suite, she gets in her birthday suit and jumps in the bed, but he sits down on the sofa and starts reading Thuh Bull. She yells, "Hey, ain't you gonna make love to me?"

He says, "I can't. Don't you know it's Lent?"

She screams, "Oh yeah? To whom and for how long?"

Say What?

Blonde goes to get her hair cut. The hair stylist cuts for about 30 minutes, hands the blonde a mirror and asks, "How do you like it?" The blonde says, "It's okay but could you make it just a little longer in the back?"

Blonde: "I was born in Georgia."
Her boyfriend: "Oh, really? What part?"
Blonde: "All of me, silly."

Once a night, every night

Once a year, every ye[ar]

THUH BULL

Let's Get MARRIED

3 Ring Buying Tips

1. Go to a store that sells things. . . *jewelry*, for instance.
2. A surprisingly great place to shop for men's wedding bands is **in their pockets** at a singles bar.
3. If she's blonde, *glass* could be a girl's best friend.

BAD WEDDING GIFTS

A beautifully framed 8 1/2 x 11 prenuptial agreement

General Tips

✔ Don't

✔ If you must marry, don't marry outside your species.

✔ Never get married at a bowling alley. Statistics show that 63% of all bowling alley marriages end in divorce. In fact, the only wedding site that has a higher subsequent divorce rate is the church.

✔ If you plan to marry a roofer, may we suggest suicide as a more pleasant alternative?

✔ Instead of rings at the wedding ceremony, why not give something more practical? For instance, we at Thuh Bull recommend that you exchange *aluminum siding*.

✔ WARNING: You can probably expect your new wife to have the 'sweat hog' syndrome if, on the way out of the church, she never lets a piece of rice hit the ground.

✔ Watch out for pranksters. At my wedding, one of my friends put 5,000 crickets in my car. Instead of the honeymoon, I did what any red-blooded male would do — I went fishing. The divorce was final 3 weeks later.

7 HABITS OF HIGHLY INEFFECTIVE PEOPLE

by **Steven Lovely**

Habit 1: Pick out a role model. . . a roofer for instance.

Start young. Don't play doctor and patient, or even cowboys and Indians. Play games like *roofer* and *furious homeowner*. Even if you don't attain the status of roofer, with such high expectations you could go on to become a highly successful *shovel leaner* on a D.O.T. crew.

Habit 2: Don't use excuses . . . unless they're darn good ones. "My *wife is having her throat amputated this morning*," will get you much more mileage than calling in with the fake flu voice and pretending you're sick.

Habit 3: Never blame yourself. For instance, your boss tells you to sweep the company parking lot and you forget. He calls you in his office and demands to know why it ain't been swept. The proper response you should give him is . . . "*What parking lot?*" If that doesn't work, divert his attention by burning down the storage room.

Habit 4: Take "Match Book Offers" more seriously. There are lots of exciting opportunities right above the "Close before striking" section of a match book. You can go to pilot school and learn to fly for about $40,000. Or, you can learn to fly by mail for only $99 (while supplies last) or you can even learn to *fly by night* for less than that. And better yet, if you don't feel good (or your wife is having her throat amputated) you don't have to call in, you can just write it in.

Habit 5: Drink beer in convenience store parking lots. This is called networking. You can meet all sorts of interesting and influential people this way. You can make important contacts with roofers, painters, Pizza Hut delivery drivers and with any luck whatsoever, an occasional Christian man, with references, who does yard work.

Habit 6: Have a goal. While you're at home waiting for a lucrative get-rich scheme or maybe an exciting match book offer to come your way, you need a goal to keep your mind off your troubles. K-mart has them starting at just $49.95 (while supplies last). Just look in the basketball section.

Habit 7: Stay healthy. With those hard-to-open pop tops, do you realize you can burn off over 90 calories just opening a case of beer? Heck, that's more calories than is contained in one entire beer! What that means is, if you drink 24 beers a day, one of them doesn't count. Two cases of beer a day and . . . well, you do the math.

Tourist Trap Automotive Garage

So you had a little problem with your car and you dropped it off at the local garage. When you come back to pick it up, your bill is $11,350. Now you quietly request an explanation since you feel the bill is a trifle high. The mechanic explains, "We were only able to salvage the radiator cap, so we just screwed a new car under it."

The Bull Wonders . . .

Why do dyslexics like to play 81 holes of flog?

Tourist Trap Drycleaners

A lady from Toledo storms into a local drycleaners and says, "So, you call yourselves the best drycleaners on the Beach." And then she throws something across the counter to the manager. The manager looks at it and says, "This washcloth looks perfectly fine to me." She screams, "Washcloth?! When I brought it in here it was a *bedspread!*"

Bubba
and Graduation Night

It was graduation night at Auburn a few weeks ago and they were about half way through the ceremony of handing out diplomas when they came to Bubba. The President interrupted the ceremony and said, "Ladies and gentlemen, we have a problem: Bubba is a few credits short and won't be able to graduate tonight."

Well, Bubba was the starting right guard for the Auburn Tigers, and when the student body heard that he wasn't going to graduate, they all jumped up and started to chant, "Give Bubba another chance, give Bubba another chance!"

The head football coach and the President have a quick conference and afterward, the President announces that they have decided to give Bubba another chance. Bubba is told he will be given a 'one question' math test and if he passes, he can graduate. The question is, 'What is 2 plus 3?' Bubba thinks for about 20 minutes and then says, "I have it, the answer is 5." There is complete silence in the auditorium for a couple of seconds and then the entire Auburn football team (they are sitting on the front row) jumps up and begins to chant, "*Give Bubba one more chance, Give Bubba one more chance.*"

The Bull Makes A Very Indecent PROPOSAL

RENT MY WIFE

BULL INTERNATIONAL HEADQUARTERS.

After seeing the movie "Indecent Proposal," I went home and asked my wife if she would sleep with Robert Redford for one million dollars. She said, "Of course I would, but you know we don't have that kind of money. . . . I wonder if he would settle for our $17,000 savings account, $350 in monthly payments and the beach house?" Well, that made me mad! But it also gave me an idea. If a rich man like Redford would pay a million dollars to spend the night with someone else's wife, surely the low-rent trailer park type men would pay $15 to $35 a night. To make a short story even longer, welcome to the Bull's . . . ***Wife Rental Company***.

Here are the models we have in stock:

1952 green-eyed brunette, 118 pounds, looks great with the top down, average size headlights, comes with own mace security system, purrs like a kitten if you put the right fuel in her. Price $29.95 per night.

1960 3/4 ton redhead, great for hauling heavy equipment, but eats fuel like it's going out of style. Can stop on a dime, especially if the dime is in front of a Dairy Queen. Only 42,000 original donuts. Needs work on the rear. Will sacrifice . . . only $9.95 per night.

1965 Blonde. Brand-new paint job, but spends a lot of time on the rack. No original equipment, but the new transmission seems to be working fine. This beauty has only 13,412 previous owners but still a steal at only $19.95 per night. Split it with a buddy.

1980 brunette in mint condition, a real "cherry" if you know what we mean . . . maybe a few dents, but no real damage. No previous owner, although every customer we have would like to test drive her. She can be had, but it's gonna cost you. One of the tightest rear ends you'll ever get your hands on. Today only . . . $89.95

YOUR LOCAL BANK

Loan Application To Borrow $5.00

Name of future debtor:_____

Address of our future property once you default on this loan: _____

Blood type: _____   Place fingerprint here

Collateral: Check as many as possible:
- ❏ Firstborn child   ❏ Future Inheritance   ❏ Your Life Savings
- ❏ Your Retirement   ❏ Everything Else (you must check this one)

Occupation (don't give us that blue collar crap) _____

Income: Check one:
❏ $250,000 a year
  (*If you **don't** check this one, we suggest robbing a convenience store for the $5.00*)

List 4,000 credit references _____
  (*You may use other side of this form if necessary*)

Questionnaire

1. Do you need the money?   ❏ Yes   ❏ No
  (*If you checked 'yes' you are through with this application. Don't call us and we CERTAINLY won't call you.*)
2. Do you: ❏ Rent ❏ Own (*If you checked 'Rent' see above*)
3. If you have worked at your present job for the past 50 years, what did you do before that?
4. If you are ever late on a payment, do you hereby give up all of your rights as a human being?
  Check one: ❏ Yes

Bonus Question

5. Our records indicate that in May of 1967, you were 15 minutes late on your $3.00 monthly Sears payment. Please attach a 20 page explanation (*do not double space*)

For Official Use
This loan has been disapproved for the following reasons:
Check one: ❏ Reason A   ❏ Reason B   ❏ Because
Signature Loan Officer _____

Ask Dr. Bull

Dear Dr. Bull,

My seven-year-old has warts on the soles of her feet. What causes this?

Grace S.

Dear Grace,

You and your child may have heard the old wives' tale. You know, the one about human papilloma virus causing warts, but actually, papilloma virus has nothing to do with it. It's frogs peeing on your kid's toes.

Dear Dr. Bull,

Okay then, what should I do about it?

Grace Again

Dear Grace Again,

Keep the little yard ape out of frog urinals.

Dear Dr. Bull,

Cholesterol, cholesterol! I'm sick of hearing about it and you can't even see it!

Lacy P.

Dear Lacy,

Wrong! Of course you can see it. Simply go to McDonalds and order a bag of fries (and no, tell them you don't want fries with that). Then lay one French fry on a napkin. Wait 3 minutes and look at the big grease spot on the napkin. That is cholesterol. (By the way, if you're into taste, forget the French fry. Just pour a little catsup on the napkin and eat it.)

How you see it   How they do it

You Gotta Read This

(As appeared in the *Los Angeles Times*)
Just How Unlucky Can One Get

Just when you think that everything that could go wrong has, you hear about someone who has worse luck. This one was faxed to the FEMA office in Sacramento.

According to the fax, authorities in California found a corpse in a burnt-out section of forest while assessing the damage done by a forest fire. The deceased was dressed in a full wetsuit, complete with dive tank, flippers and face mask. A post-mortem examination revealed that the person died not from burns but from massive internal injuries.

It seems that on the day of the fire, the person, identified by dental records, went on a diving trip off the coast. Firefighters had called in a fleet of helicopters with large buckets which were dropped into the ocean, filled and then flown to the fire and emptied.

You guessed it! After being scooped up from the Pacific in the fire bucket, he apparently extinguished exactly 5'11" of the fire.

Thanks to John F.C. for mailing us the clipping.

WHY EVERY WOMAN OWNS AT LEAST

4,000

PAIRS OF SHOES

by Ms. Bull

WHY, YOU ASK?

① Because, it'd be pretty silly to own only 3,999 pairs, don't you think?

② You never know when a complete stranger may walk up to you and ask you to kick a field goal.

③ Because, if we ever go broke, we can build a parking lot in front of our closet and open a shoe store.

④ You have to avoid that terrible fashion mistake . . . *clashing*. I once knew a woman who had only 2,971 pairs of shoes. She wore a pair to work. They clashed with the water cooler. She hasn't been the same since.

⑤ What if the Church Youth was having a scavenger hunt? They come to your house. They need a pair of blue pumps with high heels made from a left-handed alligator from Southeast Brazil, made in 1993 on the 3rd of June. What if the only pair you had like that was made from a right handed alligator? Could you live with yourself? I don't think so.

BULL THOUGHT FOR THE DAY

If a single fly can have 1,000 offspring, just think what a *married* fly could do.

"MAMA, THEY CALLED ME A SCUMBAG!"

OVERHEARD

"When I went out with Elvis, it was always a triple date — Elvis, me and his pharmacist."

Cybil Sheppard

CELEBS

WHAT'S THIS

Thanks to Honest Hal Bullard

ANSWER: *A Haitian Ocealiner.*

NOTICE

Due to the lack of trained trumpeters, the end of the world has been postponed indefinitely.

100% T-SHIRT WINNER

There were two men walking toward each other on a sidewalk . . . both dragging their left foot. As they passed each other, one guy says, "Vietnam '68." The other turns around and says, "Dog crap, 20 feet back."

Horriblescopes

by Jeanne Dixon's Little Brother . . . "Mason"

Virgo (August 23-September 22)

People born under this sign, like the great Virgo of all times, President Clinton, have one genetic defect. They were born with no skeletal system. No backbone whatsoever. I bet if a serial killer was in your house systematically taking out each of your family members, you would call 911 under an assumed name. Otherwise, God forbid, you might have to go to court and be a witness. Serial killers hate witnesses.. He might get mad at you and not be your best friend. But there are advantages to being spineless. You could be in a terrible car wreck and break your back and no one would ever know it because x-rays don't detect Jell-o.

Libra (September 23 - October 22)

When I think of you, I think of that famous hyphenated word . . . "financially-illiterate." All people born under this sign are destined to file bankruptcy. Let's look at the facts: you own a Salad Shooter, don't you? A Salad Shooter is a gadget. A gadget is defined in the Bull dictionary, page 231, line 8 as: "a thing people buy who don't have brain one; an object people pay up to sixty dollars for so they can keep it a couple of years and then sell it at a garage sale for thirty-five cents." You probably own a "Miracle Thaw" too, don't you? Look, you idiot, if God had meant for people to buy a Miracle Thaw from Mr. Ronco, he wouldn't have invented room temperature.

Scorpio (October 23 - November 21)

Your life is meaningless — that's the good news. And the bad, you ask? It will get worse. But I'm not here today to bash you, that would be too easy considering your sub-human existence. No, I'm here to review your life's accomplishments. You have never been arrested for rape. I didn't say you've never raped, I just said you ain't been caught. What else? You once came in 3rd in a pie-eating contest. . . probably still have the certificate on the wall, and ten to one that it shows up on your resume too. Very nice. Oh yeah, your biggie that you still brag about today. . . back in 1989 you were the eighth caller and won a clock radio. Put that on your resume and you'll find yourself as a management trainee in some of the finest laundromats this country has to offer. Nothing personal, but I have met part-time roofers that have accomplished more than you.

Sagittarius (November 22 - December 21)

You at the grocery store! People have been shot and killed for less. Let's take a look: when you go grocery shopping, evidently you think you're the only person in the entire free world with a digestive tract, hence, you must think you're the only one in the store. I bet you take a tape-measure so you can get your cart dead center in the middle of the aisle. And you leave it there blocking people all the way to the produce section while you check out the nutritional value on the back of a can of rat poison. And then it's off to the checkout where we all wait 2 hours and 15 minutes as you frantically search every nook and cranny of your purse or wallet to find your 25 cents off a can of rat poison coupon.

Horriblescopes

Capricorn (December 22 - January 19)

Back in January 1947 there was a Capricorn born with a birth defect. Oh, I know it rarely happens. In fact, it never happens. But it did happen once and what's worse, it happened to me. It was heart-breaking, it was gut-wrenching. You see, I was born with an uneven number of eye lashes. There! It's finally out! God, I hope all the other Capricorns don't turn against me. I had to get this off my chest. For six years I've been lying to you, telling you that I, like all other Capricorns, was perfect. Yes, I had 32 eye-lashes over my right big beautiful blue eye, yet only 31 over my left big beautiful blue eye. Oh sure, my parents had a team of surgeons fly in from around the world to correct it before I was 20 hours old, but still, I feel I let you down. I'm sorry. You may be seated. Amen.

Aquarius (January 20 - February 19)

You smoke, don't you? Don't lie to me! I've seen your lungs. Two words come to mind . . . *charred wreckage*. You smoke a lot, don't you? Has it ever occurred to you that your habit could affect the visibility over Los Angeles? How does it feel to personally affect the smog report? I bet, in your home, you go through about 3 smoke detectors a week. You said I met you once . . . actually we did meet, but at the time I just mistook you for a buck-toothed forest fire. My ex-wife used to smoke. When she was away, I missed her. No seriously, sometimes I would get so lonely for her while she was out of town, I would sneak out on the patio and French kiss a bag of charcoal. Not a lot of difference except the charcoal didn't nag.

Pisces (February 19 - March 20)

You are a pet lover, which consequently makes me detest you. Oh, pets are okay I suppose, as long as they are kept where they belong — in a pet store. But noooo, you not only have pets in your house, you let them out to prey on society. Your dog left about 3 pounds of preying on society in my front yard the other day. I missed him but that's only 'cause I ran out of ammunition. And I love it - it's about 3 a.m., I'm trying to sleep off a world-class hangover and at a time like that, there's nothing better than listening to (right below my window) a three-alarm cat fight. Why Purina doesn't make tuna-flavored cat poison, I'll never know. (Look you idiots, it's a joke, okay? I love cats! No seriously, I do. They taste a lot like chicken. Now, scram.)

Aries (March 21 - April 19)

You're always broke, aren't you? You know why? Let's see, how can I put this in a nice way . . . well, you're broke because you're basically a brain-dead imbecile when it comes to money. Let's look at the facts that I will make up. First of all, you paid perfectly good money for this Book. There is absolutely no social redeeming value to this book whatsoever, so stupid you whips out your wallet (or purse) and pays for it. You have to admit that's pretty ludicrous in and of itself. But there's more . . . you buy crap just because it's on sale. . . . "Oh, look Honey, Kmart is having their annual bird cage sale . . . buy 150 — get one free." Now you understand that brain-dead imbecile part, don't you? And finally, gasoline prices always end with '.9'. If gasoline is 99.9¢ a gallon and you give them a dollar, they owe you one tenth of a penny change. I demand it. In fact, every time I fill up. I feel it is my God-given right to get in a fist-fight with the clerk. You don't, you're stupid and that's why you're broke. Now, go away.

Horriblescopes

Taurus (April 20 - May 20)

I've been in your house before and quite naturally, I've written how disgusting it was, but the other day, I had some extra time on my hands, so I came back unannounced. Normally, when you know I'm coming, you clean it up to look like your basic landfill, but not this time. It was rude. Let me put this as nicely as I can: I honest to gosh mistook your living room for the site of a plane crash, except in this particular case, there was no possibility of survivors. And you know them NASA scientists that say they've discovered life on Mars at a cost of only 50 million dollars? Shoot, they could study the primitive life forms on your shower walls for free. And there was enough algae and mildew on the shower curtain to start a small to medium swamp. All they'd have to do is just add frogs. Now go away! Go on! Scat! Get outta my book! Shoo!

Gemini (May 21 - June 20)

When I think of you, I think of the type of people that frequent yard sales, flea markets and rummage sales. The typical person that attends these "functions" has an average IQ of about 15 percent higher than plant life, has a 4.3 year elementary school education, knows over 400 words fluently and can count to 75 without the help of others. On the other hand, you have your weaknesses too. For instance, you once had to turn down snapping up a good deal on a broken crock pot because you didn't have a 30 cent piece with you. And when you get ready to leave one of these functions you don't say something like "Have a nice day"; you say something like, "Ya'll got any jumper cables I can borrow?"

Cancer (June 21 - July 22)

I had a garage sale last week. All the people born under this sign showed up. I had a friend video the entire morning from across the street; it wasn't pretty. It reminded me of that Olympic event . . . synchronized drooling. People like you are what gave riffraff such a good name. At one time there were 37 cars in front of my house . . . the city ordinance guy came by and almost fined me for operating an auto salvage yard without a license. Diane Elko and her friend Judy were there. They must have had plans to attend every garage sale in town because between them, they must have had over 85 cents. Diane offered me 30 cents for a TV set. I yelled, "That's a rip-off!" Diane said, "No it isn't, silly, I'm talking about the new one in your living room." I fired a warning shot over her broom and she flew off.

Leo (July 23 - August 22)

Don't *underestimate* your worth, others will do it for you. Today is a good day to hone up your poetry skills. You need to get out and mingle with VIPR's . . . you know, Very Important Puerto Ricans. By the way, your spouse is having an affair with a part-time roofer but cheer up, it could be worse. It could be with a full-time roofer. You know, you used to be an attractive person, but you're recovering from it nicely. C-Ya!

THIS JUST IN

The Center For Disease Control in Atlanta said today that cancer is no longer the nation's number one killer. Now it's Jack Kevorkian.

Dear Bull,
What is the ideal height and weight for a lawyer?

Chris A.

Dear Chris,
The height should be about 6 inches, and the weight about 3 pounds including the urn.

ENTERTAINMENT NEWS

The movie "Joe's Apartment" is about a guy that lives in an apartment full of cockroaches. It has been so wildly successful they're already planning the sequel . . . "Denny's Restaurant."

It was 19 years ago that Elvis died. Investigators in the case say they're now looking into a so-called "second pharmacist theory."

USA *Today* Reports

Scientists have discovered a natural amphetamine that enters the bloodstream during sexual foreplay is also found in soda pop (true). In a related story, plans have been announced to introduce a new line of soft drinks called, "Mountain Dew Me."

***Heard on THUH Radio**.*

Republicans are a diverse group:
75% are white
20% are Caucasian
5% are honkys

PEOPLE-WATCHING AT THE MALL

You ever do it? You go to the mall, order a coffee and just watch. It's fun, I did it last Saturday. You talk about weird.

Here's what I saw

- A woman with a butt so big it took up Sears.
- 13,000 pimples and a boy that lived under them.
- An old man that walked so slow he actually lost ground.
- A baby that had evidently swallowed an air-raid alarm.

You might be a "Whimp"...

If your idea of a physical sport is full-contact piano lessons

If you are afraid of the neighborhood librarian

If you've ever sat down with a 6-pack of milk and rearranged your butterfly collection

If you've ever been beaten up by a poet

Thanks to: Curtis L.

---

2 More Tacky "Yo Mama" Jokes

1. Yo Mama is so cheap she would ask for separate checks at the "Last Supper."
2. Yo Mama is so short, you can see her feet in her driver's license picture.

WHAT'S THIS?

ANSWER: *It's what my neighbor's male dog must see every time I walk in his house.*

Amish Classifieds

035 TRANSPORTATION

For sale: 2 horse-powered wagon: beautiful barn-room condition, 38 original miles. Air-conditioned by Mother Nature. Has 2 speed transmission; slow and slower, AM 8-track tape deck for all your favorite top 40 gospel hits. Driven to church only on Sunday, Monday, Tuesday, Wednesday, Thursday, Friday & Saturday and kept in a barn. $200 or will trade for 3 new goats and a used chicken.

036 PERSONALS

Single virgin female, 48, would like to meet thou. Must be non-everything.

✪

Widowed male, 38, seeks thee. I am a social buttermilk drinker and occasionally I like to smoke. . . goats, turkeys and misc. wild game. Hobbies include building barns and tuning up buggies.

✪

Single Amish female, new to Pennsylvania, seeks professional farmer to cultivate and harvest with. My hobbies include praying, scrubbing, baking and taking long walks in the church parking lot.

040 BARN SALES

This Saturday morning come out and enjoy our 3 family barn sale. Many items available including wagon wheels, bear traps, plows, buttermilk churns and a large selection of beautiful 15 year old black frocks.

045 HELP WANTED

Ice box repairman. Must have knowledge of ice and your own wagon. Pay range from 5 to 10 bushels of wheat per week.

✪

Door-to-door vegetable sales. Experience as a Mormon helpful. Call thee and I will call thou back.

050 ENTERTAINMENT

Talk to live Amish girls wearing nothing at all but 15 or 20 articles of clothing. 1-900-HOT-AMISH.

BULL ATTENDS
WRITER'S GUILD MEETING
(True Story)

Well, as the esteemed publisher of Thuh Bull, I received a request by mail (postage due) to join a local writer's guild. I was excited! I was elated! I was an idiot.

On the first night, the speaker opened with . . . *"Tonight, we're gonna have a frank and candid discussion about the heart-breaking problem . . . abuse of semi-colons."* I said to myself, *"Okay, I have seen semi-colon abuse, let's go for it."*

But the second night, well, that was a different story. When I first got there, it was fun, I'll admit it, everybody sitting around drinking a few ice-cold RC colas and telling their favorite punctuation joke. But then, as the night drew on . . . .

Read below some things I observed:

• One man got up and gave a slide presentation about the advances in exclamation points, compete with accompanying music. You talk about thrilling!!! (Always use 3 exclamation points after the word *thrilling*.)

• We learned how to talk about the heartbreak of sentence fragmentation with a loved one.

• One lady spent 9 years in England studying paragraphs. Much to my surprise, the perfect paragraph is 89 words long, not 88 as had previously been thought.

• We learned how to spell 4-letter words using the miracle of punctuation marks. For example, if you want to write dirty words without being caught, you could write — "Well, you can just kiss my &!@:!" instead of using the "A" word.

• Then we started talking about margins. You'd be surprised to learn so many interesting things about 'left-handed margins.'

• Then, as the meeting ended, they asked me if I would like to join the Writer's Guild for only $300 a year. Naturally, I told them to BITE MY "?@#$" and went home.

WHAT'S THIS?

ANSWER: *The sign advertising beer huggies.*

WHAT'S THIS?

ANSWER: *An Old Milwaukee in an Alabama beer huggie.*

OLD PEOPLE NEED MORE TO OCCUPY THEIR TIME

They like to complain so we're here to help.

- Close every left lane in America.
- Have Doonesbury do the daily obits.
- Sneak into the parking lot of a Sunday afternoon shuffleboard game and put "My Grandchildren Bite" bumper stickers on all the cars.
- Close Florida during the winter.
- Make all yard sales start at 11 o'clock at night.
- Put all pharmacies and complaint departments on the centerline of interstates.
- Make it illegal to keep your turn signal on over 2 hours and 15 minutes in expectation of a future right-hand turn.
- Put white socks and sandals at opposite ends of Wal-Mart.
- Require all letters to the editor to be one word or less.
- Tax wrinkles.
- Require a 3-year cooling off period before tee times can be issued.

Nine Out Of Ten People
Are Rejected As Game Show Contestants!

Chicago, Ill. — Fortunately, it's not as bad as it seems. Yes, right after they are rejected, they are bussed over and get to be audience members of the Oprah Winfrey Show.

THE NAME GAME

The redneck couple kept having children. Finally after quadruplets arrived Pa looked at his wife and said, "Ma, I think we have 'bout run out of names. I can't come up with anything to call these four boys."

"Well, I can," Ma replied, "Adolph, Rudolph, Get Off and Stay off."

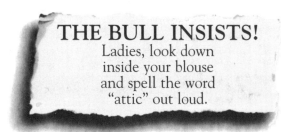

THE BULL INSISTS!
Ladies, look down inside your blouse and spell the word "attic" out loud.

More Handy PUT DOWNS

☛ Nice hair! You must give me the name of your clown.

☛ Do you feed your chins separately?

NEW JERSEY
Can Be Dangerous To Your Kid's Health

Is New Jersey really as dangerous as they say? Yes, the infant stores up there are now offering bullet-proof vests in pink or blue.

WEATHER FORECASTER MURDERED

In Boston yesterday, a popular TV forecaster was found murdered in his apartment with a note reading . . . "Yesterday was the last time I'll ever shovel 2 feet of partly cloudy and warmer temperatures out of my driveway."

Your page 72 waiter would like to serve you this joke.

The greatest naval battle in Mexican history was kept secret until the recent Mexican elections. It occurred between Mexico and the Japanese in 1938. The Mexicans lost 15 battleships, 2 atomic subs, 9 aircraft carriers and 13,341 men. If you think that's bad, you should have seen that Japanese fishing boat!

BULL Factoid

Accidents aren't so bad! After all, they cause more people than they kill.

BULL POLITICAL QUESTION

If Bill, Hillary, Al and Tipper were all in a boat that sank, who would be saved first?

A. *The US Economy*

Believe It Or . . . Believe It

If you would like to see 7 million b...holes wrapped in plastic, just go to New Jersey and ask everybody to show you their driver's license.

How a dyslexic reads the above signs.

TOP **5** ALABAMA TOURIST ATTRACTIONS

THUH BULL

⑤ THE WORLD'S LONGEST DIRT ROAD

See 984 miles of breath-taking potholes on the world's longest dirt road. Located from one end of Alabama to the other.

④ SIX FLAGS OVER OPP

An amusement park for the whole family, especially if your family is blind because Opp is the most God-forbidden dipstick of a town I've ever seen.

③ THE JOHN DEERE MUSEUM OF MODERN ART

See a stunning array of fifteen million used tractor parts, all arranged in alphabetical order for your viewing pleasure. Children over 12 admitted free.

② THE BOILED PEANUT MALL

Visit 375 acres of boiled peanut stands under one roof. Spend the day sampling every kind of boiled peanut known to man including fried boiled peanuts, baked, barbecued, sauteed, marinated, smoked, frozen and even boiled boiled peanuts. Plenty of free tractor parking and they even have a big porch to keep your dogs on.

① HUBCAP WORLD

Visit the world's largest side of a barn tastefully decorated with 425,010 hubcaps. A must for the whole family. Free admission to children under 0. Located on the side of every dirt road in Alabama.

TOP 10 LIST

(Why Letterman Should Hire Thuh Bull)

10   I need the job 'cause my two inventions flopped . . . mail-order oil changes and prescription Saran Wrap.

9   And funeral confetti ain't doing too good either.

8   Because I have in my possession an original document that says, "You're a lot funnier than Letterman, Love Mom."

7   'Cause my girlfriend has a world-class tush (How did that one get in here?).

6   So I can legitimately use that world-famous "I write for Letterman so get in the truck, b...h." pick-up line.

5   Because I can spare the 23 seconds it would take to out-write his current staff.

4   Because I am the acting president of the "Leno Bites" fan club.

3   Do not adjust your paper. This reason is temporarily out of order.

2   'Cause I'm a black, handicapped, dyslexic, homosexual, left-handed female so you have to hire me.

1   I can write funny 'cause I don't use ink in my pen, I use *clown's blood*.

WHAT'S THIS?

$$\frac{x}{x\text{-}ski}$$

ANSWER: *A Polock co-signing for a blonde.*

HAVE YOU BEEN MURDERED YET?

Cereal Killer Trading Cards

Miami, Florida. Well, it's gotten so bad in Miami that even the kids are swapping "Serial Killer" trading cards. (see right) But wait, there is hope for Miami. No, you idiot, not hope as in wishful thinking, hope as in Bob. . .Bob Hope. Yeah, because of all the crime and violence in Miami, Bob Hope is going there to entertain the police.

BULLTEST

Which word (or words) doesn't belong in the following sentences?

• After winning 32 bikini contests in a row, *Time Magazine* acknowledged that Julie "has the finest set of jumper cables in America."

• Oh yeah, we forgot to tell you. Julie is now working at a restaurant that has an owl for a logo and their slogan is . . . "more than a mouthful." As we all know, the name of that restaurant is "Jumper Cables."

• After the driver tailgated me for 15 miles, I finally had enough and slowed down to two miles an hour. When he finally passed me, he shot me a fried chicken!

OOPS!
OUR APOLOGY

The BULL says "we're sorry" for last month's issue in which we printed the chest measurements of the Swedish Bikini Team on the front page instead of the figures of the *1975 Annual Soy Bean Sales* to former Soviet Republic.

Those Hilarious Amish
Things they do and say. . .

❦ An Amish teenager was pulled over by a State Trooper in Ohio last week and charged with having too much *buttermilk* on his breath.

❦ Amish shoplifters are different from normal shoplifters. They sneak into the store and put things back.

❦ An Amish father came home one night to find his wife shot, his daughter raped, his son beheaded and his barn burnt down. He was so P.O.'d, he looked up toward the sky and yelled, "Dag Nabit!"

❦ And there was the Amish farmer who's horse and buggy got 5 hours to the mile.

❦ Barbara Walters was interviewing this old Amish couple and she asked, "So you've been married 63 years. During that time, how many times have you had sex?"

The old Amish gent snapped, "I already told you, we have *two* kids!"

"So that means you've had sex twice?" she asked.

"No, you idiot, what do you think my wife is, promiscuous? They are *twins!*"

Letter From Florida "Gator" Student To Friend

Dear Joe,

Just a few lines to let you no how its going down hear at the yun . . . uneiver . . . universet . . . uneiver-set . . . school of Deleware.

I finally bought a used car. The guy drove it around the world backwards 3 times so it only has 15 original miles on it. He only wanted $300, but I gave him $2,000 for it because I needed a more reliable car.

I had A's in all my classes right up til the semester started. My teachers all asked my parents to send excuses for my presence, what ever that means.

Our football team is really good. We crushed our apponets last weekend, 3 to 0, for our first win in a row. The other team cheated anyway. They didn't show up til the 4th quarter.

I am supposed to take something called calculus next semesster but I don't think I will. Heck, I don't even like broccoli.

My girlfriend is a cheerleader and she has a great bod. I can't wait to meet her.

The food at the school cafeteria isn't that good. I don't understand because they cater it from the hospital.

Well, I don't hear someone knocking at my door, so I better go see who it isn't.

Yore fiend,

X

P.S. I lost your address, so call me when you don't get this letter.

POLICE BEAT

by Detective Sgt. Bull

(This column is dedicated to our fine law enforcement officers who deal with scumbags everyday. If you know one that kills a dirtbag in the line of duty, please send us his or her name and address so we can award them our highest award . . . the Bull's Purple Bullet of Honor. They also win $5.00 in cash and a Bull "I Killed a Scumbag" t-shirt.)

Some people get all bent out of shape for nothing. Like for instance, this time this woman got her panties in a wad just because I had shot her husband for not using his turn signals, or the time I beheaded a shoplifter during a blue light special at Kmart. Nevertheless, I have mellowed out some since my early days. Let me tell you about my first encounter as a cop back in 1973.

I was a rookie, fresh out of the Police Academy and ready for action. I was assigned to the worst part of town. The Chief knew I had personally blown away 1,700 Viet Cong during 'Nam and he figured I could take the heat of battle.

How could I be so lucky. The very first night I'm cruising down the interstate in Jacksonville when a cement block comes crashing through my windshield. It had been thrown from an overpass. Things like that tend to upset me. After all, not only had it killed my partner, but it spilled my coffee and smashed my free do-nut that I had just picked up at a convenience store.

I knew not to turn on my blue light because I was in a seedy part of town and all the dirtbags would run out thinking I was a portable Kmart. Dirtbags just love blue light specials. I looked up at the overpass and saw 3 illegal aliens making a run for it. I could tell they were illegal aliens because they were spray painting the overpass as they ran.

As my patrol car and I raced to the exit ramp where the 3 scumbags were, I could see them trying to start their $50 car. The battery was dead (actually it wasn't dead, but like I say, who's writing this garbage, you or me?) so they figured they were caught. They came walking up to me with their hands up. The first one yelled, "Ortego Sanchez Taco Hut" or something like that. I think it's Spanish for "We surrender."

I thought to myself . . . "B.S. you say! If I arrest them, they'll spend about 6 months in jail on manslaughter charges and be out on the street again ruining free coffee and donuts in no time." So naturally, I put 15 bullet holes in each of their heads. Just then an eye-witness appeared. I thought, "Oh crap, this ain't good." I asked him his name and what he had seen. He said, "My name is Danno, I work for the Hefty Trash Bag Company and what I saw was the fact that you need 3 free samples." With that look in my eye that Danno (who later became an officer and my partner) would come to know and love, I said, "Bag 'em, Danno."

Footnote: The Chief saw the 15 bullet holes in what was left of the dirtbags' heads and said it was the clearest case of suicide he'd ever seen.

DOOR-TO-DOOR NO MORE!

Are you sick of Avon ladies, Girl Scout cookie saleschildren, Buffalo's Witnesses, all kinds of misc. zeros and pinheads coming around door-to-door trying to sell you some crap you don't want?

How To Answer Your Door

1. Partially close one eye.
2. Come to a full drool.
3. Stick your tongue out the side of your mouth.
4. Open the door, point to your ear and say, "Num, knee nigh, knee num naw." (repeat if necessary)
5. Begin shaking your hand loosely (as if you've burned it and you're fanning it.)
6. Close the door.
7. That's it. They will never come back, period!

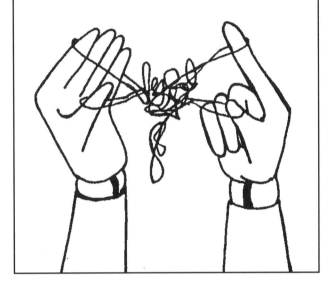

GI Joe, sure he was pretty handy with his rifle — but he sucked at cat's cradle.

You know it's a slow news day when!

When they open the news broadcast with some author being interviewed about his block-buster novel, **The Complete History of Helium.**

Note *to all virgins:*
"Thanks for nothing!"

101 Brunette Jokes
OR BLONDE REVENGE

1. Why do brunettes like their dark hair color?
Answer: It doesn't show the dirt!

2. Who make all the bras for brunettes?
A. *Fisher-Price*

3. What do you call a beautiful brunette?
A. *A Rottweiler*

4. Why didn't Indians scalp brunettes?
A. *They discovered the hair from a buffalo's butt was much more manageable.*

5. How do you get a brunette to say "yes" on the first date?
A. *Ask her to marry you.*

6. Why are most brunettes flat-chested?
A. *It makes it easier to read their T-shirts.*

7. Why are brunettes so proud of their hair?
A. *It matches their mustache.*

8. If blondes get fingers run through their hair, what runs through a brunette's hair?

A. *Lice*

9. How can you tell the color brunette is evil?
A. *You ever see a blonde witch?*

10. Is it true blondes have more fun?
A. *No, they have **all** the fun.*

11. How can you tell a brunette is lonely?
A. *Check her for a pulse.*

12. What is the most frustrated animal in the world?
A. *A brunette rabbit.*

13. Why do brunettes wear training bras?
A. *Because it's cheaper than changing their bandaids every day.*

14. Why was the first football stadium sketched out on a brunette's chest?
A. *Because they needed a level playing field.*

15. Why did they quit selling brunette Barbie dolls?
A. *Parents felt the dandruff might be contagious.*

16. Why do brunettes sleep

all night on their stomachs?
A. *Because they can.*

17. How do brunettes get the tangles out of their hair?
A. *With a rake.*

18. What one thing can really screw up a brunette's day?
A. *A mirror.*

19. What is the official color of Poland?
A. *Brunette*

20. How do you drown a brunette fish?
A. *Just add water.*

21. What do you call brunette twins doing bubble gum commercials?
A. *Double-dumb.*

22. What's so good about brunette midgets?
A. *They're only half as ugly.*

23. What do you call a brunette with no hair?
A. *A bald-headed idiot.*

24. What would the photograph of a brunette say if it could talk?

101 Brunette Jokes cont.

A. Yes.

25. What did the brunette say to the U.S. Marines?
A. Yes - 350,000 times.

26. Why did the brunette chicken cross the road?
A. Because there were 14,000 roosters on the other side.

27. What kind of costumes do little brunette kids wear on Halloween?
A. They don't, they just stand on their heads and go as dirty mops.

28. Why don't brunettes get breast implants?
A. They already spent their money on thigh implants.

29. What did the frustrated brunette say to her uninterested lover?
A. "Just what part of the word 'yes' didn't you understand?"

30. Why did God create brunettes?
A. So ugly men wouldn't be left out.

31. How can you spot a flock of brunette geese?
A. They're the ones walking south for the winter.

32. Where do you find a brunette bat?
A. Laying dazed on the ground next to the side of a barn.

33. What do brunettes miss most about a great party?
A. The invitation.

34. Where do brunettes get their black hair?
A. It's transplanted from their underarms.

35. Do not adjust your book. Joke #35 is temporarily out of order.

36. Why do brunettes have to pay an extra $2,000 for a boob job?
A. Because the plastic surgeon has to start from scratch.

37. What do many brunettes wear on their face that matches their hair?
A. Warts.

38. If a blonde and a brunette jumped off a skyscraper, who would hit the ground first?
A. The blonde. The brunette would stop along the way and beg somebody to marry her.

39. What does a brunette look for all her life and then just dies when she finds one?
A. A gray hair.

40. How do you describe a brunette whose phone rings on Saturday night?
A. Startled

41. What do you call a good-looking man with a brunette?
A. A hostage

42. Why did God create brunettes?
A. Because He screwed up and created the "old maid" category first.

43. Do not adjust your book. Joke #35 is temporarily out of order.

44. How did Revlon come up with its brunette hair color?
A. By studying what oil spills did to seaweed.

45. Why can't brunettes "tease" their hair?
A. Because it's not funny.

46. How can a brunette get lost in a crowd of three?
A. It's easy. . . if one-third of the crowd is blonde.

(cont. on page 129)

BULL Factoid

Eighty percent of married men cheat in America. The rest cheat in Europe.

NEWS IN (MY) BRIEFS

☛ After losing only 28,000 lumber related jobs in the Northeast, efforts to save the spotted owls have been wildly successful and both of the owls seem delighted also.

FAMOUS QUOTE
"Give me ambiguity or give me something else."

The BIG ONE Gets Bit!

6 Signs That You Have Gone To A Bad Funeral Director

1. There's a Domino's Pizza logo on the side of the hearse, and they drop off a couple of pizzas on the way to the cemetery.

2. He asks if you want cremation "original" or "extra crispy."

3. Gives you a souvenir t-shirt reading, "My beloved spouse passed away, and all I got was this lousy t-shirt."

4. Gives you a business card for his second-hand *eyeglass* and *denture* shop.

5. Tells the bereaved, "I'm pretty sure your uncle is in Hell by now."

6. You find he has replaced your loved one's ashes with Folger's Crystals.

BULL MARKETING AWARD!

Tommy T. of T. T. Chevrolet wins this year's award. Tommy says, "Hey folks, forget about wasting your hard-earned money on eyeglasses and contact lenses . . . all our cars come with pre-scription windshields.

Rule of Life # 91
Suicide is the most sincere form of self-criticism.

Smart Cop?

This dumb butt wanted to become a state trooper. He graduated the academy, and his third night out, he came across a really bad pile-up. He freaked, called in to dispatch and said he didn't know what to do. The dispatcher told him to stay calm and write down everything he saw.

He started walking around and he wrote, "Body in the road." Then he wrote, "Body in the car." Then he saw a head in the boulevard. He wrote, "Head in the bov. . . bolev. . boiv. . ."

Finally, he looked around and seeing no one looking, kicked the head and wrote, "Head in the ditch."

BULL Factoid

It is a proven fact that the hardest job in the world is selling "**No Soliciting**" signs door-to-door.

Bull Research Pays Off!

The Bull Research Department just made an important discovery: If you eat a meal cooked in a microwave oven, you have to wait only about 30 seconds before going swimming.

BULL Factoid

One-seventh of your life is spent on Monday.

It seems that every month we destroy an area of the rain forest equal to the size of New Jersey. Wouldn't it be a lot easier to just destroy New Jersey?

WHAT'S THIS?

ANSWER: *Howard's Stern*

MORE LETTERS TO THE JANITOR

Dear Janitor,
Since rednecks clean their fingernails only once or twice a year, where would you suggest they clean them?

Homer Lone

Dear Janitor,
How do they get rid of the garbage in Georgia?

Paul B.

Dear Janitor,
Since you are a history buff, tell me, what were the first supplies that the Iraqis ordered for the Gulf War . . . more scud missiles or nerve gas?

Colon Pal

Dear Janitor,
What is your definition of a Peeping Tom?

Jill

Dear Homer,
Over a flowerpot.

Dear Paul,
They put it on the menu in Alabama restaurants.

Dear Colon,
Actually, neither. The first thing they requisitioned were 3 million white handkerchiefs.

Dear Jill,
A window fan.

WHAT'S THIS?

ANSWER: *The T-shirt GOD wears ever time he thinks about people from Alabama.*

WHAT'S THIS?

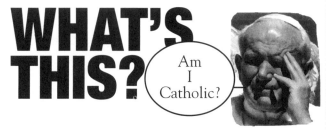

Am I Catholic?

ANSWER: *What the Pope said when asked if he thought O.J. was guilty.*

The Lighter Side of
BLIZZARDS

✳ New Jersey had its annual Shriners "Snowball Fight" in downtown Newark. Thanks to greater safety measures and the traditional holiday spirit, only 117 people were killed and, surprisingly, less than a thousand were critically injured.

✳ It was believed to have snowed 3 feet an hour in a Polish neighborhood in the Bronx, but it was later discovered that over 60% of that total was dandruff.

✳ Washington D.C. solved its snow removal problem the old-fashioned way. They gave Mayor Marion Berry a straw and told him it was just real cold cocaine.

TOP 5
PICK-UP LINES

① Do you believe in love at first sight . . . or do I have to walk by again?

② Tomorrow morning, do you want me to call you, or nudge you?

③ Do you have a quarter? I promised I would call my mother as soon as I fell in love.

④ Pardon me, I seem to have lost my phone number. Can I borrow yours?

⑤ Your legs must be tired because you've been running through my mind all night.

THE BLONDE JOKES ARE BACK

*100% brand-new, still in the box, never been read before Blonde Jokes
from your friend and mine, Thuh Bull.*

Q. Y'all heard about the blonde who wanted to commit suicide? She couldn't decide whether to electrocute herself or take sleeping pills. How did she do it?

A. She compromised . . . she took 8 flashlight batteries and swallowed them with a glass of water.

Q. How can you tell if your submarine was manufactured by a blonde?

A. It's a canoe full of big rocks and a snorkel.

Q. Did you hear about the prince who tried a glass slipper on the foot of a blonde Alabama Cinderella?

A. Athlete's foot ate his hand off.

Q. Did you hear about the blonde who tried to whitewash the fence?

A. She was rather unsuccessful, possibly due to the fact that the fence was constructed of barbed wire.

Q. How do you recognize a fashion conscious blonde on the North Pole?

A. She'll be the one wearing pierced ear muffs!

Q. Did you hear about the blonde weather forecaster?

A. On the morning news she said, "I think it's a nice day out there, but it's so foggy I can't tell!"

Q. How many blondes does it take to wash a car?

A. Thirty: one to wipe and twenty-nine to spit.

Q. Why don't Alabama blondes wear bikini swim suits?

A. It's too much of a hassle shaving their stomachs.

Q. Can a blonde beat an egg?

A. Yes, but only if she cheats.

Q. How do blondes wring out their laundry?

A. They run it through the typewriter.

Q. Y'all hear about the blonde who wanted to play records?

A. Unfortunately, she couldn't afford a new needle for her can opener.

Q. How does a blonde scientist study a vacuum?

A. She turn her head inside out and then shoves it under a microscope.

Q. Y'all hear about the blonde scientist who spent 12 years searching for the abominable snowman?

A. She brought back 5 bags full of frozen dandruff.

How The Fight Started

After a very trying day at the office, the husband was enjoying his pipe and reading the evening paper. His wife, who was working on a cross-word puzzle, suddenly called out, "John, what is a female sheep?"

"Ewe," replied her husband . . . and that's how the fight began.

MACHO BULL Factoid

In Cuba, "Whatever floats your boat" is not a saying, it's a building plan.

The following incredibly funny story was typed with disappearing ink.

MARCH
Calendar Factoids

4 **1957:** A used car salesman in Indiana was caught telling a truth and was promptly fired.

19 **1913:** Leaning Tower of Pisa is declared straight, but the rest of Italy is crooked.

20 **1931:** Bill Elevator invents the elevator. Had he known about elevator music, he said he would have invented something else.

22 **1918:** The first participle was dangled.

27 **1964:** Ringo Starr orders two beers and the peace symbol is born.

28 **1964:** Paul McCartney orders one beer and another symbol is born.

Parents ARE STUPID!

Most parents are dumb when it comes to raising kids and other family stuff. My parents were smart. Here's stuff they did. . . .

* Most kids get put on restriction and have to stay home for a week. Restriction is supposed to be a fun time for parents, so why do they make the kids stay home? My Mom would take my key, give me 137 bologna sandwiches and tell me not to come with a 25 mile radius of our house for a week.

* My Dad told me to go cut the yard. I said no, so he made me cut the entire neighborhood. After that I cut the yard - once even on a voluntary basis.

* When my Mom yelled, "Suppertime" she meant it. Be there in 30 seconds or don't eat. I lost 55 pounds before I got the concept.

* When my Dad got out the belt, he, unlike

most parents, was honest. He would just smile and say, "This is gonna hurt you more than it does me."

* My Mom used to say, "Now eat everything on your plate or you may not leave the table." I once spent an entire summer looking at a plate of 90-day-old spinach. Now I believe her. Today if she would prepare a nice barbed wire fence casserole, I would just get a bottle of catsup and my wire cutters and go to it.

* My Dad wanted to teach me right from the start not to spend money foolishly. Most parents spend over $3,000 at the hospital delivery room. Not my Dad. I remember the day I was born. It involved 2 aspirin for Mom, a pair of Sears Best pliers and some Vaseline.

* Most parents spend $75,000 just to raise one kid to adulthood. My parents did it for $85.13.

PARENT CLASSIFIEDS

Snot-nosed, whiny 6-year-old for sale or trade. I've had it with this little crumb cruncher. Answers to the name of "Shut-up and Take-a-bath." Marked down to 5% below original hospital bill.

FOR SALE

Two unidentical twins, ages 4 and 5. All they do is crap and eat and destroy things. Other than that, they are wonderful. Will consider trading for a used lawn mower or $75 in cash.

Sweet affectionate 15-year-old female for sale. Has been on the telephone for the last 3 years. Her mother hates her because we haven't been able to order a pizza since 1994. 50% off this weekend only and then 90% off after that.

EASY MIKE'S USED CHILDREN

Over 35 models in stock, all colors, all sizes. Absolutely no warranty. 90 seconds same as cash.

Special this week — 1990 Cry Baby . . . $400

FOR SALE BY OWNER

A 1987 Mouth with an 8 year old boy attached. Has eaten us out of house and mobile home. We now live under an overpass. Free to loving parents. . . no; make that 'free to anybody.'

WHAT'S THIS?

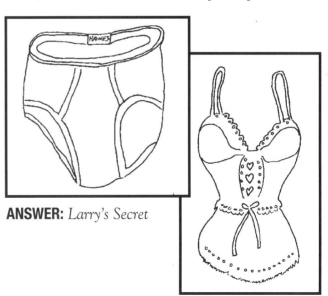

ANSWER: *Larry's Secret*

ANSWER: *Victoria's Secret*

Ceptember ateth, 1997

Mr. Stu Pid
Dorm #6
Auburn, AL

Dear Stu,

Things are really happing hear at the Pid trailer hold. Your brother was kilt in a 3-tractor collision last week but don't worry, it wasn't his fault so no points were charged on his revoked drivers license.

Your sister finally got herself pregnant and the boy agreed to marry her. In fact he gave her a beautiful ring with three stones missing.

We moved last week and had a little troubel with the bed. The man wouldn't let us take it in the taxi. But that's okay, it probably would have woken your father.

Our new next door neighbors have a 30 thousand acre pig farm. We got wind of it this morning.

Pa bought me a new imported dress from Idaho last week at Fredricks of Montgomery, but I had to take it back because it still had 3 potatoes in it.

Boy it's been hot this year but your good ole Pa figured it out. When it gets too hot in the trailer, Pa turns on the heater and then we all go outside to cool off. If he weren't such a good stock boy at Winn Dixie, he could have been a great rocket scientist.

Well, I better go, Uncle Junior bought us a garden hose for our 50th wedding anniversary and the service man is here to help us install it.

Love,
Mother Pid

P.S. People sure are dumb. Last nite a reporter for the Farm News Channel asked your Pa what he thought about them high gasoline prices. Pa said, "Heck fire, the price of gas here in Troy has been the same for the last 35 years. Depending on which pump you choose, it's either 87, 89 or 93 cents."

ever WONDER ???

? How come China gets to pick all the names for flu?

? Should you wash a dirty goldfish?

? If people don't have an American Express Card, do they have to stay home?

? What if you're not ready when Delta is?

? How do possums know to cross the road at exactly the wrong time?

? Do deaf people tell "blind people" jokes?

? What if a mosquito bites someone with a blood-type that doesn't match its own?

? Does a dog really think he can get our leg pregnant?

? Are there instructions on how to read "The Book Of Instructions"?

World Class BUBBA Story

Story of Bubba commanding his first ship in the Coast Guard: It was a dark and stormy night. . . . Bubba saw a ship approaching and had his man signal the ship to 'give way.' He was very surprised when he ship signaled back, 'No, you give way.' Bubba immediately hollered to his signal man to reply, 'I'm a Lt. Commander in the United States Coast Guard. I repeat, give way!' As the two ships drew closer and it became apparent that a head-on collision was imminent, the approaching ship signaled: 'No, you give way.' By this time Bubba was furious. As a last resort Bubba finally signaled: 'Move your vessel! I'm a 52-foot Coast Guard cutter!' The other ship signaled, 'No, you move your vessel. I'm a *lighthouse.*'

Then there was the divorce attorney who sent out five hundred perfumed valentines signed, "Guess Who?". . .

IN & OUT

About four years ago, no, it was yesterday. Anyway, this Mother Skunk has two kids named In and Out. One day she told Out and In to go out and play. Later she called them and Out came in but In stayed out. Mama told Out to go out and bring In in. Out went out to find In, who was lost. But Out told his Mom that it was no problem, he could find In in no time, which he did. So Out and In came in and Mama Skunk asked Out how he found In so quickly and Out said, "It was easy Mom — In-stinct."

Question TIME

Q. What do you call a cross between a giraffe and a German Shepherd?

A. A watchdog for the 8th floor.

Definitions:

Dust: Mud with the juice squeezed out.

Wind: Air in a hurry.

Flight Schedules: Something airlines use to base their delays on.

☞ THIS JUST IN

With all the bullet holes and airplane damage at the White House nowadays, the Clinton's are afraid when they have to move, they won't get their security deposit back.

👓👓👓

"Federal Study shows sex causes birth defects!"

"Adopt-A-Terrorist"
CAMPAIGN OFF TO GOOD START

Washington D.C.—Sally Struthers is at it again. She said she finally realized that there are over 8 million starving out-of-work terrorists in the Middle East alone and she says they need our help. Below is just 1 of the millions of poor, sad starving terrorists stories:

Rajeed comes from a broken terrorist home in South Lebanon. His father divorced his mother after she accidentally blew her private parts off as they were sitting around the Christmas tree 2 years ago making home-made chocolate cookies and pipe bombs.

Rajeed has killed hundreds of people in his short career but he made that fatal terrorist

mistake, he forgot to claim responsibility on his resume, hence his application for terrorist work has been consistently rejected.

Rajeed needs your help. Send 50¢ a month and we will send you a loving portrait of Rajeed blowing up a school bus for your home or office (suitable for framing). He will even write you threatening letters once a month.

BULL Factoid

The Kennedy children were the only kids in the world who could kiss their Onassis.

GOLFERS

The PGA is considering approving the use of hail size golf balls.

DO-IT-YOURSELF

......!!!!!!!!!???????,,,,,,,,,,;;;;;;;;;;;;;;:::
""" """ """ """

Missing punctuation in this issue.

Ann Bullanders

****

Is love at first sight really possible?

Dear Ann,

You said in a recent column that it was impossible to fall in love at first sight. Well, you are stupid. Here's my story: I had a blind date with 'Ed' three hours ago. He came to the door and said, "Hi, I'm Ed, will you marry me?" Naturally I accepted, we rushed down to the Justice of the Peace and were married. We came back 20 minutes ago and I got pregnant. I decided to write this while Ed is smoking the customary cigarette. It has been a wonderful 3-hour relationship and Ed promises to fulfill my every dream. Oh yeah, he doesn't have a job because, as he says, people just don't understand him. So there, Ann, I proved you wrong again.

Robin W.

Dear Robin,

You need to wake up and smell the toast burning. Read on sister.

Dear Ann,

I am blind so naturally I've never fallen in love at first sight, but I must admit, I have fallen in love at first smell. Once I even fell in love with one of them scratch-n-sniff packets in the middle of a magazine. Silly me.

Helen Keller

Dear Helen,

I thought you were dead.

Dear Ann,

I was sitting in the north end-zone at the Super Bowl when suddenly I spotted Sally sitting in the south end-zone, a mere 150 yards away. Our eyes met and immediately I fell in hate. Yes, it was hate at first sight. After the game I stabbed her to death. I still don't know about love at first sight, but I am living-proof and Sally is dead-proof that two people can fall in hate at first sight.

Chris

Dear Chris,
Thanks for sharing such a heartwarming story.

Dear Ann,

I recently went to a Bikini Contest at a local nightclub. If fell in love at first sight 23 times in 4 minutes. You are right Ann, anyone can fall in love at first sight.

Mark S.

Dear Mark,
No, I hate to disagree, but you fell in heat. Ten to one says at least one of your parents was a rabbit.

THIS JUST IN

Walt Disney has had absolutely no success with it's mega hit, "Aladdin" in New Jersey. Fortunately they called Thuh Bull for advice and we suggested they re-release the film in that state under a different name. . .

"Yo, Rub This!"

My Favorite Joke (on this entire page)

A woman whose husband has just died is meeting with the mortician before the service.

"Would you do me a favor?" she says. "When my husband passed away, he was wearing a brown suit. I always hated that suit, but he looked great in blue, is there still time to bury him in a blue suit?"

"Actually, yes," says the mortician. "We're doing another funeral this afternoon. The other man was just about your husband's size. He was wearing a blue suit, and I'm sure his family won't mind if we simply switch outfits."

After the burial, the mortician comes up to the widow. "I hope everything was all right," he says.

"Oh yes" she replies, "it was a beautiful service. And I was amazed to see how quickly you were able to change Malcolm's suit."

"To be perfectly honest," replies the mortician, "we were running a bit late. So, instead of changing the suits, I just switched the *heads*."

I Miss COMMUNISM

As you all know, Thuh Bull figured out why the Soviet Union went down the toilet. It was simply a matter of statistics. Here are those statistics one last time:

The Soviet Union had:
312,420,000 population
12,859,000 square miles
68 languages
5 time zones
1 loaf of bread
But . . . I sure miss them.

Here's 4 reasons why:

1. Remember the bumper stickers — 'Russia Sucks'? Well, now if you want one, it has to be 8 feet long to get all the country names on it . . . Armenia, Lithuania, Siberia, . . . sucks!

2. My Dad works for Rand McNally, the map and globe manufacturer. He left for work in April of '89 and hasn't been home since. Oh, he's okay, just real busy. For instance, he redrew Yugoslavia 12 times just last month.

3. I can no longer use the threat of nuclear warfare to get my kid to eat all her tuna casserole.

4. My brother is a grain farmer in Iowa. He used to get $42,000 a month to not grow grain. Then Russia had a food shortage and our government paid him $50,000 a month to grow it and ship it to Moscow. Now with the USSR splitting up into 32 countries, he has to fill out 32 different invoices instead of just one. He has decided all the extra paperwork just ain't worth it. He's gonna go back to not growing it and take the $8,000 a month pay cut.

DEAR FLABBY,
A COLUMN WITH REALLY *BIG* ADVICE

Dear Flabby,

I am a 4'2", 396-pound female who cannot turn down Twinkies. Flabby, we're not just taking plain old cottage cheese thighs, we're talking large curd. I recently received an invitation to our family reunion next Tuesday, and would really like to go if I can lose 275 or 276 pounds by then. Can you help me?

Signed,
Hurricane Huge-o

Dear H.H.,

Get real. Go to the reunion. In fact, you ARE the reunion. Just stay away from the BBQ pit when you have an apple in your mouth.

Dear Flabby,

My wife has gained over 500 pounds since we married last Fall. I want to take her on the honeymoon we could not afford back then and she wants to sail the Caribbean. The only problem is, I can't find a boat that will stay afloat with her on it! What should I do?

Signed,
My Honey's Moon Is Sinking Us

Dear Honey's Moon Sinking,

Your signature line gave me a great idea. Forget finding a boat to float her because a barge couldn't hold your babe. Make HER the boat! Don't worry, she'll float. Just roll her into the water, turn her on her big belly, stick a sail and mast somewhere (use your imagination) and sail 'a broad.' Bon Voyage!

TOURIST HELP:

Miami International Airport To Install Coin-Operated Cemeteries

Miami, Fl. — *"Don't let a simple murder spoil your vacation plans."* That's what the Director of Operations at Miami International Airport is telling foreign tourists. Let's say you rent a car at the airport and sure enough, 15 minutes later someone blows your wife's head off. What to do? No problem, drop what's left of her off at your local airport morgue. Put in $1.25 for 24 hours of cold storage and you're right back to enjoying beautiful downtown Miami. Also, handy accessories can be bought in the airport gift shop such as body bags, toe-tag key chains, dry ice (for the flight back home) and those great novelty t-shirts, "My Wife Was Blown Apart In Miami And All I Got Was This Lousy T-Shirt.

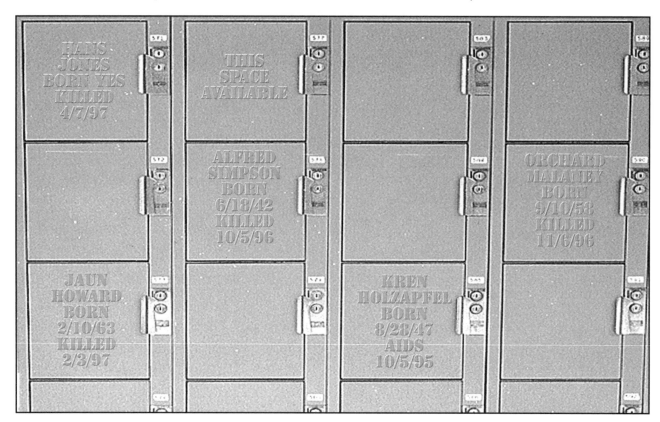

Shown above are the handy cold storage units at Miami International Airport. For just $1.25 a day, or the 2-week special of only $14.99, you can keep a loved one packed on ice while you enjoy the hospitality of South Florida.

LETTERS
To The Redneck Times

Dear Redneck Times,

I want to be the world's biggest redneck. Any suggestions?

Joseph S. T.

Dear Joseph,
Yes, instead of a buckle, might we suggest wearing a nice 114 lb trailer hitch on your belt?

Dear Redneck Times,

I was just wondering, what do you call it when you have 50 female pigs and 50 male deer in a pen together?

Shannon A.

Dear Shannon,
"A hundred sows-n-bucks."

ever WONDER ???

1. Why do Kamikaze pilots wear helmets?

2. Do test tube babies have belly buttons?

3. Does "if at first you don't succeed . . ." apply to skydiving?

NEW ways to relieve S T R E S S

• Right before throwing it about 30 feet in the air, butter your cat's feet to see if it will help him land on his back.

• Call an Olin Mills sales representative during "his" supertime and try to sell him a camera.

• Write your own obituary and mail it to the local paper. Then sit back, relax, and enjoy the flowers

BULL PERSONAL MESSAGE

To the guy driving the Consolidated Freight semi on I-10 last week, "Thanks, but I already know I'm number one."

THUH BULL

MORE *(I get minus respect)*

RODNEY DANGERBULL

☞ My teenage daughter, Brandy, is so embarrassed by my car that when I take her to school, I have to drop her off in our front yard. She walks the rest of the way. Fortunately for her it's only 17 miles.

☞ A Mormon knocked on my door. When he saw me he pretended he was selling used battleships door-to-door and left. I was lonely. I probably would have ordered a couple.

☞ My Aunt Sue called. I answered the phone. She said, "I thought you were dead,' and hung up.

☞ I used to be handicapped. I couldn't find a handicapped parking space so I pulled into one of "theirs" - you know, a regular space. A guy yelled, "Hey, you can't do that!" and stuck 75% of my wheelchair up 90% of my butt.

HEAVENS TO NASCAR!

When Davey Allison arrived at the Pearly Gates he saw his friend Alan Kulwicki waiting for him. They talked a bit and Alan said, "I've got something to show you."

Alan took Davey down a corridor and into a room. There sat the #7 Hooters T-Bird. "Wow, is there racing up here?" Davey asked. "All the time. Here, let me show you something else," Alan said. He led Davey down a second corridor into another room. There sat a shiny black #28 T-Bird. Davey said, "This is great. Are there other racers here?"

Alan led him down a third corridor into another room. Inside the room was a shiny #3 car with the Goodwrench logo. "I didn't know Dale was up here," Davey said.

"He's not," Kulwicki said. "That's God's car."

Redneck
Joke of the
Month

There were three guys on a plane going from Florida to New York on business. The first, wearing a suit and tie, reading the *New York Times* commented, "Last night I made love to my wife three times. This morning she made me fresh ground coffee, brought the paper to me in bed and said I was the best lover in the world!"

That ain't nothing," said the next guy, reading *USA Today*, dressed in Chino's and a casual shirt. "I made love to my wife four times last night. This morning she made me bacon, eggs, grits & coffee and said there wasn't a stud like me on the planet!"

They both looked at the third guy reading *Thuh Bull*, wearing jeans and a "Hooter's" t-shirt. "How many times did you make love to your wife last night?" they asked.

"Once," came the reply.

"Ha, ha, haw! And what did she say to you this morning?"

"Please don't stop!"

Thanks to Adam J.

OVERHEARD

JANE: You're going on a diet? Why?

FAT SWEAT HOG WITH A LISP: Because I'm thick and tired of it.

MISC. B.S.

● According to CNN, people who are 10 pounds overweight are now considered in style. That means my ex-wife is now about 4 times more in style now as she was last year.

● Dudley Moore just turned 61 . . . what Dudley lacks in talent, he makes up for in height.

● PBS says 30% of the world depends on rice to survive . . . they didn't have any statistics on 'Roni.'

How to tell if you live in the "hood"

☞ If it ever gets so rough outside on Easter Sunday that the preacher just faxes you the sermon.

☞ *If, when cooking a roast and you find it too tough, you can just hang it out the window for five minutes and let the stray bullets tenderize it.*

☞ If you've ever been approached by a door-to-door person selling discounted graffiti lessons.

☞ *If the neighborhood axe murderer moves away because it's just not safe anymore.*

☞ If the car insurance costs you $375 per month . . . and that's just for full-coverage on a set of keys.

Thanks to Buck D.

POLICE *BEAT*

by Detective Sgt. Bull

It was *not* a dark, stormy night but since I'm making this crap up it *was* a dark, stormy night. My partner Danno and I had hit it big. Since we led the Police Dept. in killing or wounding dirtbags while on duty, we got our choice of patrols. What officer wouldn't want the . . . Trailer Park Patrol. What a great way to spend a Saturday night!

Our Captain had told us it would probably be a slow night; after all, it was Christmas Eve. I knew better; many dirtbags that live in trailers view Christmas Eve as a fine time to get a little domestic violence out of their system. I mean, after all, they have the whole family gathered in one room around the Christmas tree.

Danno and I were slowly cruising through the Down and Out Trailer Park admiring the stained mattresses leaning upside the trailers and all the fifty dollar cars in the driveways when, sure enough, we heard gunfire. Oh sure, we had heard 40 or 50 rounds fired off period-ically through the evening, but this was differ-ent. Kids were screaming, "Dad, don't kill Mom! She didn't mean to lose your jumper cables!" Danno looked at me and said, "You were right, Bull, old man Batson is at it again."

Charlie Batson and I went way back. I sent him to the Big House in '84 for child abuse and manslaughter because he convinced some panty-waste judge that when he killed his step-son, he had meant it in a nice way. I knew he would kill again if **someone** didn't stop him. I looked in the rearview mirror and saw **someone**. I'll be darned, that **someone** was me. Tisk, tisk.

I pulled out my toy cap pistol. I had used it so many times before. It was my secret weapon, and the main reason I led the nation in dirtbag killings. As you may know, an offi-cer can only return fire if fired upon. Sometimes you need to encourage the dirtbag to fire first. Toy cap pistols usually do the trick.

I told Danno to cover me as I waded through the empty beer cans to the front door. The violence was heating up inside. I heard a little girl yell, "Please, don't drink anymore, you've already had 37 Old Milwaukees." I could hear the child's face being hit with what sounded like a fist, or maybe just an old used coffee table. It was showtime.

I opened the rusty old trailer door and yelled,

POLICE BEAT CONT.

"Hey, dirtbag, it's Thuh Bull! Listen to this!" Then I fired off 6 rounds of my cap pistol. Batson figured I had emptied my revolver. He grabbed his .357 and came charging out the front door like an old drunk cow. He fired right at me but since I'm writing this garbage, he missed wide right (kinda like an Auburn place-kicker).

I took aim with my deer rifle and then stopped. I figured what the heck, I'll just put in some hollow point bullets (the type that could blow an elephant into 15,00 little tiny elephant pieces from a thousand yards out). I took aim and squeezed off 1 round . . . no, what the heck, I squeezed of 25 rounds.

When it was all over, there was nothing left of Batson but part of that nasty old fish net tank top he always wore. I suppose I had gotten carried away but maybe I'll get over my guilt. There, I'm over it.

Danno got out of the car bringing with him a Hefty 30-gallon garbage bag. With that familiar twinkle in my eye that Danno had seen so many times before, I grinned and said, "Bag him, Danno."

Danno laughed out loud for 15 or 20 minutes. When he could finally contain himself, he looked at me and said , "Bag what?"

I just smiled and said, "Nothing but *net*."

BULL SALUTES
MAD MAGAZINE

In a recent issue of Mad, they did a deal on corporate mergers. Go buy one, it's good. The best was - 'What if Macy's merged with the Trojan Company? Answer: Some of the most memorable Thanksgiving Day Parades in history.'

So naturally, Thuh Bull will try our hand at it.

WHAT IF . . .	RESULTS
Delta Airlines merged with Greyhound?	Buses that hit the side of mountains
R.J. Reynolds merged with Smokey Bear?	Low-tar forest fires
Exxon merged with Wal-Mart?	Cheaper oil spills
U.S. Postal Service merged with Fed-Ex?	Guaranteed lost mail by 10 o'clock the next morning.
What would you get if Harley-Davidson merged with Midas Muffler?	A Honda
Rolex merged with General Electric?	A $10,000 alarm clock
Mercedes and Yugo?	A car that won't get you there . . . in style
What if AT&T, MCI and Sprint merged?	We could have gone a long way in ending TV violence
Motel 6 and Motel 8	Motel 14 (are y'all dumb or what?)

BULL
Hangover Remedy

First take the juice from two fresh cans of beer...

An unusually dangerous stretch of Interstate 10 for the Possum family.

A tribute (of sorts) to

F I R E M E N

☛ Firemen are strange people. When little Bobby Elko was a kid, he couldn't wait to grow up and roast marshmallows over a nice, warm, burning apartment complex.

☛ Firemen tend to brag. Chief Bobby Nichols of Bear Creek VFD told me the other day not to worry about burning in Hell. He said if he got there before me, he'd go ahead and put it out.

☛ For entertainment, a firefighter will often have some of his buddies over to have a few beers and watch a nice forest fire on TV.

☛ Firemen are weird too. After putting out a house fire, they will go home and tell their kids cut little bedtime arson jokes.

☛ All firefighters must first attend a Smokey Bear Blow Out My Zippo Training School. Bob Elko graduated first in his class and has since gone on to put out 12,352 Bics in his illustrious career.

Thuh Bull's Exercise And Diet Rules

✍ Do one sit-up a month whether you need to or not (You should start noticing a difference in your waist-line in less that 35 years.)

✍ About 3 times a week, blink on purpose.

✍ After eating a 23,000-calorie meal, listen to a Weight Watchers commercial.

✍ Once a week, hold your stomach in for 10 seconds even though nobody is looking.

✍ Before eating a gallon of ice cream, always **white-out** the "fat" content.

✍ Once a year, actually drive by a Dairy Queen without putting on your turn signal.

✍ Eating chocolate chip cookies in the dark doesn't count against you.

✍ On the 3rd Friday of every month, do something drastic and hide the remote control from yourself for 3 hours (we suggest having a doctor or nurse standing by during this one).

✍ Go on a self-imposed 12-minute hunger strike.

BULL INTERVIEWS Mrs. Dahmer

Bull: "Tell us Mrs. Dahmer, were there any early signs that your son, Jeffery, would end up to be a serial killing cannibal?"

Mrs. D: "Well, as I think back on it, maybe there were. When little Jeffery was 3 years old, he ate our neighbor's cat."

Bull: "Did you spank him?"

Mrs. D: "No, you see, I don't have any arms."

Bull: "What happened to your arms?"

Mrs. D: "I don't really know, I just woke up one morning and all I had left were two bloody nubs."

Bull: "You don't think . . . "

Mrs. D: "No, no, Jeffery was always such a sweet boy, but maybe a trifle strange."

Bull: "What do you mean, 'a trifle strange'?"

Mrs. D: "Well, at Thanksgiving, he always insisted we have cranberry sauce and a baked spleen."

Bull: "Where did you manage to buy spleen?"

Mrs. D: "I didn't, Jeffery always brought them home. Well, actually, we didn't always have spleen; sometimes Jeffery would bring home various organs — a pancreas, maybe a nice 8-pound thyroid gland, you know."

Bull: "Didn't you question where these 'things' came from?"

Mrs. D: "Oh sure, but Jeffery always assured me they came from the final clearance sales down at the local morgue."

Bull: "Did Jeffery have many friends when he was growing up?"

Mrs. D: "Yes, but for some reason, they all would only come around 2 or 3 times and then stop."

Bull: "How about the recent developments. Jeffery is accused of killing, dismembering and eating 17 young boys. How can you possibly explain that?"

Mrs. D: "He always did have a great appetite."

BULL
Historical Fact

In 1897 an Alabama man invented the toilet seat.

In 1908 a Georgia man put a hole in it.

Thanks to Marie P.

MORE
'How FAT Was She?'

▶ She was so fat she couldn't fall down a flight of stairs because some of her was already there.

▶ She was so fat she couldn't wear soccer cleats because she kept striking oil.

▶ She was so fat she began developing her own ozone layer and weather patterns.

▶ She was so fat that when she wore her 'Malcolm X' jacket, a helicopter mistook her for a landing pad.

Thanks to Mark R.

BULL
MONEY $AVING TIPS

$ To save wear and tear, every other day, wear your clothes inside out.

$ Cut down on iron pills and eat more paper clips.

$ When you go on vacation, forget to feed your animals. No one will know but the animals.

$ When your tuna casserole has been in the refrigerator for 3 months sell it off to the local elementary school as a science project.

$ Save your dead batteries. They work great in broken toys.

$ Tell your friends and relatives to go to $%#! Unnecessary doorbell ringing from unwelcome visitors can run your door bell electricity expense up as much as 12 cents a year in some major metropolitan areas.

$ Don't buy Sprite. Just throw one-tenth of an Alka Seltzer in a glass of ice cold rain water. (You won't be able to tell the difference. Other people will be able to tell you're an idiot, but that's beside the point.)

"Mid-East World"
TO OPEN SOON!

Just when you thought you'd never get to see a car bomb attack in person, Disney World has signed an agreement with 17 Mid-Eastern countries to bring all the action-packed fun of the Mid-East right here to a theme park in America.

WHAT YOU CAN EXPECT:

✤ You'll die with laughter at the front gate of Mid-East World when you see little signs like "Enter At Your Own Risk" and "Insure Yourself A Good Time By Insuring Yourself For The Last Time."

✤ Participate in a real-life soccer riot and join in the fun by actually getting 3 of your front teeth knocked out.

✤ Don't be disappointed by the long lines in front of our most famous attraction — The Tacky Iraqi — because every 15 minutes a car bomb will go off right before your very eyes, thus eliminating about 50 percent of the line.

✤ Watch in air-conditioned comfort as three Libyan generals behead a man because he didn't go to the Mosque but 19 times last Sunday.

✤ Volunteer one of your family members to take the ride of his/her life on El Air Airlines and watch it be blown out of the sky. (Mid-East World recommends that you choose your most unpopular family member for this ride.)

✤ Enjoy our 35,000 square mile desert where you can see such beautiful things as sand . . . and even more sand.

✤ Visit Mid-East World's gift shop, Ayatollah's Foot Locker, where you can purchase such intriguing gifts as a basket you can carry on your head the next time you have to evacuate the homeland and walk 4,000 miles to the next country. Or how about a nice Iranian T-shirt that says, "America Bites!" right on the front?

✤ And to end your day, sit around a campfire with those fortunate enough to make it through the day, roasting marshmallows and singing anti-American protest songs. (Mid-East World will even give you a nice U.S. flag to burn too.)

Y'all come back now, ya hear?

BULL PUBLISHES
Clinton's Secret Phone Number

Every morning about 7:35 (CST) President Clinton jogs down to the McDonald's Restaurant located at 175 17th Street in Washington, D.C. Since you can't get in touch with him through the White House, we suggest you call McDonald's and just leave them a message to give to Bill. Their phone number is 1-202-828-8311.

Y'all Voted For Him

A tourist went into a Florida gift shop to pick up some souvenirs. She picked up a photo calendar of President Bush and saw that the price was $5.95 plus tax. She saw a photo of Reagan and the price was $4.98 plus tax. Then she came across a photo of President Bill Clinton and the price was $6.95 plus tax, plus tax, plus tax, plus tax.

More Ways to Relieve TENSION

❶ Yell "Movie!" in a crowded fire station.

❷ Cut yourself in half and then see which half of you can get a date with a midget first.

❸ Send an "I'm sorry your well" card to a hypochondriac.

CHICAGO BITES!

I swear this is true. The night after the Bulls won the NBA Championship, they interviewed a Chicago cop who described the aftermath celebration as "peaceful violence." The looting was contained to only a 36-mile radius, there were only 173 arson cases reported and best news of all, only 2 people were killed. I called the families of the two victims, and they were overjoyed also.

Bull Family Secret REVEALED

I was the 17th of 23 children. The reason there were so many of us was that my mother was hard of hearing. That is true. At bedtime every night, Daddy would say to Mama, "You want to go to sleep or what?"

Mama would say, "What?"

BORN LOSER

Kenny was born with one major problem . . . stinking feet. He tried everything even washing them (Kenny was from Auburn you know). Anyway, no matter what he tried, his feet smelled horrible.

One night while on vacation at the beach, he was feeling lonely and depressed so he decided to go out to the local club, LaFeelya, and drown his sorrows.

It just so happened that Susan was there that night to escape from the reality of her major problem . . . bad breath. Her medical bills were in the thousands, but to no avail. Her breath could back a bulldog off a plate of guts.

Anyway, they met and with all the smoke and other smells, both of them were able to hide their problems from each other.

One thing led to another and they ended up in Kenny's motel room. He went into the bathroom, scrubbed his feet, poured aftershave on his socks, wrapped them in a towel and came to bed.

Susan then went in the bathroom brushed her teeth, drank half a bottle of mouthwash and came to bed. As Kenny was lying there nude with the sheet wrapped around his feet, Susan climbed on top of him and said, "Kenny, I've got a confession to make." "I know," he said, "you ate my socks."

BULL CALENDAR Factoids

1977: On this date, TV dinners were banned in Alabama. Too many people were choking on the picture tube.

1991: Ripley's Museum opened on this date in China but they changed the name to Ripley's Believe It Or Else.

1965: Cuban television began state-of-the-art election coverage. They went out in the streets, counted the dead bodies and projected a winner.

COLLEGE BASKETBALL TEAM
LOSES 106 IN A ROW!

A division 3A college team, the Pioneers of Camden, NJ, haven't won a basketball game in 4 years. Why? We set our team of one reporter, Mr. Farking Bastage, to find out. Here is his report:

My Report:

* The team has only one basketball to practice with. As their coach put it, "This is New Jersey, for crying out loud! We use all our money for the important things of life." When I asked him to give me a for instance, he said, "Ammunition."

* Due to the embarrassment of losing, no self-respecting coach will go there, so quite naturally, before each game they a call up Rent-A-Coach.

* The height of the team is 7'6". But when you divide that by five. . . .

* So they always have a winner at homecoming, they don't schedule a game, they schedule a scrimmage. . . . That didn't always work though. Last year's homecoming game ended in a tie . . . 0 to 0. Twenty-two overtimes and 5 hours later the game was finally settled with one lucky toss. Not with a basketball, with a *coin.*

* The local newspaper saves time by printing their win-loss record a year in advance.

Mr. Farking Bastage

* The cheerleaders don't use pom-poms, they use surrender flags.

* They have a $3.00 admission price at the gate. Yep, and if you bring a friend, you get $6.00.

* Once the Pioneers were trailing 184-06. Their coach called a time-out, got his players together and said, "Don't give up, there's still plenty of time left. In fact, we've still got 13 minutes and 55 seconds." A player asked, "In the game, coach?" "No, you idiot," he said, "in the first quarter."

Dear Bull,

I would like to set the record straight, I am addicted to alcohol, not sex. So what do you think about that?

Michael Douglas
Hollywood, CA

Dear Michael,

I'd say you were missing half the genetic structure that would make you a Kennedy.

I'm About Sick of Blonde Jokes, but. . .

Q. What's the difference between a blonde and Federal Express?

A. One costs about $10 and absolutely, positively delivers overnight, and the other is in the package shipping business.

USED CAR SALESMEN NEED OUR HELP!

Think about it — a used car salesman wakes up in the morning, looks in the mirror and says, "I need some new lies. It takes me an average of 47 lies to sell one used car and I'm afraid my customers have heard them all."

Okay, Bull readers, we need your help. If car people can't sell cars, they go on welfare, our economy goes down the tubes, first thing you know, the whole nation is in shambles. All because used car salesmen ran out of lies. Help save our nation! Send in some new lies. To give you an idea, I just drank a 37-pack of Old Milwaukee and thunk up the following lies . . . but it's not enough.

SAMPLE LIES:

☛ "Good mileage? Shoot, this '82 Chevy still has the original gas in it."

☛ "Is our warranty *lifetime*? Heck, better than that. Many people that buy here list their warranty as part of their estate. That way it can be inherited."

Things About

Women's Hair

① Women spend 83% of their time talking about hair. Actually, that's not true, bald-headed women talk about hair only 74% of the time.

② My ex-wife has tried everything on her hair . . . she has washed it, dried it, vacuumed it, ironed it, heck, once she even had it dry-cleaned. She said she wouldn't do that again — she had one heck of a time getting the safety pin and that little orange tag out.

③ Hair spray. Y'all ever read the various degrees of "hold" on a can of women's hair spray? "Regular," "Super," "Extra-Super," "Super Extra-Duper, Will Withstand A Category 5 Hurricane," and "Steel Reinforced." No wonder my daughter keeps a garden rake in the bathroom.

④ You ever smell a woman's hair after a permanent? I'm not sure, but I think it smells like fried ammonia.

It Wasn't PRETTY

So this blonde sees the freight train coming and speeds up to beat it across the tracks.

The investigator at the scene of the accident wrote on his report, *"Some idiot, racing to beat the train, died when she hit the caboose."*

YOU'RE WHAT?

An Iowa farmer had just planted a huge crop of corn, and fearing the Polish crows would eat it, he stuck a giant scare crow in the field. He awoke next morning to find the crows tearing the thing to bits, screeching and throwing straw in every direction. This went on for weeks. Everyday the farmer built a new scarecrow and every day the birds destroyed it. Soon the corn began to grow and the attacks diminished. Seeing a wary crow in a nearby tree, the farmer asked:

"What's the matter? Did you birds finally give up?"

"Heck no!" exclaimed the crow. "We're afraid of corn!"

WORST COLLEGE FOOTBALL RECRUITING PICKS

⑤ **Tommy "The Rope" Poindexter**, 98 pounds, 7'4", Q.B. Graduated 3rd in his class from a major, Mid-Western charm school. They call him "The Rope" not because he can throw one, but because he looks like one.

Strong areas: Dressing out
Weak areas: Football
Achievements: Tommy was tackled only once his senior year, primarily because he is so tall and skinny. When a big ol' linebacker would be about to tackle him, Tommy would quickly turn white from fear, lay down and disguise himself as the 50 yardline.

④ **Leroy "Ax Man" Smith**, 492 pounds, 4'3", Right Guard. Played out of Valdosta High. "Ax Man" got his nickname when fellow teammates would come up and ask him if he knew his father and he would always reply, "Don't ax, man."

Strong areas:
Week areas: Everything else
Achievements: Came in second in the 40-yard dash . . . everybody else tied for first. "Ax Man" once gained 62 pounds . . . not during an off-season, during a halftime.

③ **Dil Bert**, 178 pounds, 6'2", Linebacker. Played 1/2-A ball for the Rhode Island Methodist Men's Club. Dil Bert doesn't have a nickname so the players just call him "Dilbert."

Strong areas: During a tense goal-line stand, has been know to belch the other team off-sides.
Weak areas: Very uncoordinated, once tripped over the 35-yardline.
Achievements: Spends the off-season practic-

BOTTOM 5 LIST CONTINUED

ing synchronized humming. Sings in the football choir. Has never met a fumble he didn't make.

❷ **Biff "Hands" Nichols**, 138 pounds, 5'9", Free Safety. Plays out of San Francisco High. "Hands" got his nickname because his hands are everywhere, especially down the other team's uniforms.
Strong areas: Has a sweet smile. Has been know to flirt the other team off-sides.
Weak areas: After he tackles an opposing player, he holds them down while he does their hair.
Achievements: Redecorated his team's locker room in pink with a nice teal accent. Also nominated himself as the team's shower monitor.

❶ **John "The Tub" Zardinski**, 714 pounds, 4'9", Offensive Line. (No, he's not *one* of the offensive line, he *is* the offensive line.) Plays out of the Colorado Culinary Institute in Denver.
Strong areas: Has one of the best appetites in high school football.
Weak areas: Like to paint himself yellow and disguise as a school bus in the stadium parking lot.
Achievements: The only player in high school history to have ever eaten a fumble.

TEST YOUR BLONDE KNOWLEDGE

1. What do blondes use condoms for around Christmas time?
   A. Safe sex
   B. Water balloons
   C. To gift wrap bananas

2. What do you call blonde twins?
   A. Best friends
   B. Sisters
   C. Identical idiots

3. Why don't blondes like to cook vegetables?
   A. It takes too long
   B. Their mama didn't teach them how
   C. According to most blondes, it's too hard to get them out of the wheelchair

4. What is a blonde's favorite color?
   A. Pink
   B. Red
   C. A light shade of clear

5. Why don't blondes like buttered toast?
   A. It's too fattening
   B. Too much starch
   C. They can't figure out which side the butter goes on

6. Why did the blonde make love in the microwave?
   A. She was weird
   B. She was cold
   C. She wanted to have a baby in 9 minutes

Answers
   Correct answer: C
   If you got 6 right you are probably me.
   If you got 5 right you are average.
   If you got 3-4 right you drool a lot, don't you?
   If you got 1-2 right you are braindead.
   If you got 0 right you are blonde.

THUH BULL STAYS AT THUH

HOTELS • RESORTS • SUITES

Yep, I sure did. And two weeks later I got a letter from Bill Marriott. (True) He sent me one of them "*Customer Satisfaction Surveys.*" It asked me questions like the ones below:

1. How did you enjoy the cappuccino machine?
2. Did you like the imported French mints on your pillow?
3. What is your opinion of our new 18th-century paintings on the bedroom walls?

So that gave me an idea. I went to Motel 6 1/2 and spent a night. Sure enough, 2 weeks later I got a "*Customer Satisfaction Questionnaire*" from Tom Modett. Here it is.

MOTEL 6 1/2
"Leaving the Lights on for America for over 15 Years"

Customer Satisfaction Questionnaire

1. How many roaches did you have to kill during your stay at Motel 6? Check one: ___100___500___A bunch

2. Why didn't you steal our Motel 6 towels? Were you embarrassed to let people know you stayed with us? Check one: ___Yes

3. How many burnt out light bulbs were in your room? Check one: ___One___Both of them

4. Did the drug deal going on in the adjoining rooms hinder your sleep? Check one: ___Yes

5. Is this the first time that you've ever stayed in a motel room that didn't offer T.V. remote controls?
   Check one: ___Yes___No

6. Is this the first time that you've ever stayed in a motel room that didn't offer T.V.s either? Check one: ___Yes___No

7. Would you be willing to pay extra if we ever do decide to put telephones in the room? Check one: ___Yes___No
   Why not?___

8. Were you shot at in the parking lot? Check one: ___Yes___No

9. Don't lie to us! Was anybody wounded? Check one: ___Yes

10. Do you like the radio commercials with our president Tom Modett? Check one: ___No, they suck.

11. To save expenses, you didn't really mind bringing your own toilet paper did you? Check one: ___Yes___No

12. No? Well, how about the sheets and pillow cases? Check one: ___Yes___No

13. How long did it take for room-service to get your heater to work? _____

14. There you go again! We don't have freakin' heaters!

15. Would you ever stay at a Motel 6 again? Check one: ___Yes___No

16. Why not?

17. Even if it was free? Check one: ___Yes___No

18. Well, then, bite us!

Bull's Hurricane *WIND* Chart

WIND STRENGTH	DESCRIPTION OF OBSERVED EFFECTS
Category I **74 mph**	A good stiff breeze. Great day for flying well-constructed kites. Bad day for flying well constructed airliners. Great conditions for seeing the latest in female underwear fashions. Probably too windy to play golf, or badminton. If you must play something, we suggest horseshoes.
Category II **89 to 110 mph**	Tie down small pets and lawn furniture. Do not let your kids go surfing unless, of course, you have them heavily insured. Kite-flying conditions are marginal. Small birds will be seen doing bird tricks, like flying backwards.
Category III **110 to 129 mph**	You will begin to notice that things you never thought could fly actually can, like, for instance, aluminum siding and small farm animals. If you must play golf, play downwind and use less club than you think you need. During a category 3 Hurricane in Key West last year, a golfer teed it up and hit a 7-iron shot to Indiana. Unfortunately, he 3-putted for a bogey.
Category IV **129 to 149 mph**	If you insist on flying a kite or something, we suggest just tying a string to a dumpster? Like magic, trailer parks begin turning into parking lots (Who says hurricanes are all bad?). If you go outside, you will begin to notice little pieces of debris stuck to your head, like small rocks and maybe even an occasional garbage can lid.
Category V **149 mph plus**	Small-to-medium size apartment complexes start dancing merrily through the air. Forecasters recommend moving to higher ground, say Mt. Everest, for instance. High-rise condos will begin taking on the appearance of just your basic run-of-the-mill plane crash. If you stay inside, your hair will blow off. If you go outside, your head will blow off.

And When It's Over

| **Category 0**
5 to 7 mph

Breeze, Partly Cloudy, a beautiful sun-shiny day! | An outpouring of help from around the nation. People rush in from hundreds of miles away to sell one dollar bags of ice at only $25. How thoughtful! Laborers fly in to help rebuild. Get your roof put back on for almost less than what your house cost in the first place. And looters volunteer to help carry away those unwanted TVs and VCRs. Yes, it's a beautiful day in the neighborhood. . . . |

A Poem To Myself

I like myself, I think I'm grand,
When I go to the show, I hold my hand.
I put my arm around my waist,
When I get fresh, I slap my face.

ONE SMART BOY!

A couple had been married for 15 years, and one day the husband decided he was going to get an answer he wanted to hear. When his wife came home from shopping, he handed her two aspirins and a glass of cool water and waited for a reply. His wife said, "Honey, I don't have a headache." Then he said very calmly, "Gotcha!"

BULL'S TOP 4 LIST
(Of Things A Gay Army Captain Might Say)

4. "Okay, men, tonight I'll lead you in an armed panty raid behind enemy lines."

3. "I can't wait 'til they give us those cute little military-issue earrings."

2. "I think I'll go out and tidy up the battlefield."

1. "I don't care about a promotion, but flowers would be nice."

Handy Put Down For A SWEAT HOG

"You're the perfect weight for somebody else's height."

103% TRUE

Question: When is the safest time to drive on the freeways of Los Angeles?

Answer: From 8:15 'til 8:45 on Saturday morning. That's when all the other drivers are loading up with ammo.

Thanks to Ed

Women of the '90s

The woman and her husband interrupted their sightseeing to go to a dentist.

"I want a tooth pulled. I don't want gas because I'm in a big hurry," the woman said, "so just yank the tooth out as quickly as possible and we'll be on our way."

The dentist was quite impressed. "You certainly are a courageous woman. Which tooth is it?" The woman turned to her husband and said, "Hey, dipstick, show him the tooth."

OVERHEARD

OVERHEARD AT A MAJOR OIL STRIKE IN TEXAS

Worker: Wow! I've never seen so much oil! We must have hit the motherload.

Foreman: Naw, better than that. I think we've struck Puerto Rico.

BULL MILITARY QUIZ

Q. Who has more military experience than Bill Clinton or Newt Gingrich?

A. Shannon Faulkner.

One Last Blonde Joke

It was 'Blonde Night' on *Wheel of Fortune* and they tried to make the puzzle as simple as possible with a fill-in-the-blank. . . . Old McDonald had a _____ .

Pat asked contestant number one to fill in the blank and she said, "Tractor!" Wrong response, so he asked blonde contestant number two and she said, "House!" Wrong again, so he asked contestant number three and she scratched her pretty little platinum blonde head for about 5 minutes and finally blurted out, "Farm!" Correct answer! "Now," Pat said, "for an extra $500, who can spell *farm?*" And all 3 blondes jumped up and said, "E . . . I . . . E . . . I . . . O!"

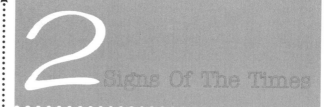

2 Signs Of The Times

Seen in Nashville: A homeless man on a street corner had a sign that read, *"Will Coach Vanderbilt Football for Food."*

Seen In Vietnam: A sign on a restaurant that said: *"Beware of dog, we didn't filet them properly."*

OVERHEARD

Grocery Bagger to Customer:

"Do you want to destroy a tree by using paper or endanger the environment by choosing plastic."

The Beverly O.J.'s

(sung to the tune of "The Beverly Hillbillies")

By Thuh Bull

Come and listen to my story
'Bout a man they call O.J.,
Rich and black and famous
And football he could play.

He could really run through air-
ports,
And jump with all his might,
But all he ever wanted,
Was something soft and white.

(Nicole that is, white girl, big
lungs.)

So he axed her this question,
"Will you marry me?"
It'll be all wine & roses
And domestic violence free."

Nicole said, "Yes" to O.J.
And it was really a lot of fun,
Except for all the time she spent
Dialing 911.

Finally Nicole had had it,
She said, "Enough is quite
enough.
Get your butt in here,
And pack up all your stuff!"

(Divorced that is — See ya!
History)

Well, the next thing you know
Nicole and friend are dead,
Seems someone attempted
To remove her pretty head.

Police head straight to O.J.'s
But they have to climb the fence,
There's no sign of Simpson,
Just tons of evidence.

(Bloody gloves, that is, blood
samples — DNA)

Police call O.J.'s lawyer and say,
Bring him to the station,
But that interferes with O.J.'s
plan
For a permanent vacation.

Yes, O.J. was escaping
And what was to be a raid
Turned into a world-class circus
And a made-for-TV parade.

(Prime time that is — Bronco
Commercials — 70 million viewers)

On his first day in jail,
O.J. said, "this place sucks!
I think I'll buy a verdict,
They're only 5 million bucks."

So O.J. bought an attorney,

In fact he bought him ten,
And all the media called it
An easy O.J. win.

(Piece of cake that is, justice for
sale — System gone haywire.)

After 6 months of trial,
The foreman had his say,
"Your Honor I'm proud to
announce,
We reached a verdict today."

So Judge Lance Ito asked,
"Well, what's it going to be?"
So the jury foreman smiled and
said,
"Set the boy free!"

(Autographs for the jury, that is,
movie deals, interviews)

Well, it cost O.J. millions,
And a very pretty wife,
But at least he hid one asset —
A bloody 10-inch knife!

The End

Bull Unclassified Ads

265 BUSINESS OPPORTUNITIES

EARN $600 A WEEK. **UNSTUFF ENVELOPES AT HOME.** Yes, for years we have helped hundreds of you stuff envelopes in the comfort and privacy of your own home. Well, now they are all stuffed so it's time to start unstuffing them. Send $75 and proof of purchase from a box of cat litter and soon you will be on your way to untold wealth and financial security.

ever WONDER ?????

During all the wars America has been involved in, why are we always the VISITORS? What about the **home country advantage**? We should have held the Vietnam War in New Jersey.

BULL Factoid

Contrary to what dyslexics think Thuh Bull does not "Make Fat of Fun People."

LIAR CONTEST WINNER

I was fishing and ran out of bait so I looked around and saw a book with a picture of a worm in it so I tore it out and put it on my hook and threw it in the water. A couple minutes later I caught a 8 x 10 inch glossy of a trout.

HOW UGLY WAS SHE?

Well let's just put it this way, if ugliness were tar, she could be the interstate system.

BULL HUNTING TIP

If you aren't having any luck duck hunting this year, maybe you aren't throwing the dog high enough. Duh!

The Actual Phone Call

Have you ever read those little notices on the side of consumer products? Well, every one of them has a toll fee 1-800 number you can call with your questions and comment. We at Thuh Bull called 5 of the numbers with our questions and comments.

(This is 1 of only about 3 true stories in this entire Bull.)

Here are excerpts from our call to the manufacturer of Windex. We called their toll free number at 1-800-558-5252 with our questions.

"S.C. Johnson and Son, how may I direct your call?"

"I have a question."

"Please hold. (Pause) Hello, Consumer Services, this is Mary, how may I help you?"

"Yes, I have a friend that says if you mix 1 part ammonia with 10 parts water and throw in some blue food coloring, you have your own homemade Windex for about 1/20th the cost. Is that true?"

"Sir, we are not allowed to discuss competitors' products."

"Competitor? He ain't no competitor, it's just Rufus Watkins down at Luther's Garage."

"I'm sorry sir, do you have any more questions?"

"Yes, who do you think will win the Sugar Bowl?"

"I would have to assume that FSU will stomp Florida's butt."

(Actually, she didn't say this. We just put it in here to see if you were paying attention.)

"Sir, we don't deal in sports predictions, only wax and glass cleaner."

"Okay, what ingredients go into Windex?"

"I'm sorry, sir, we aren't allowed to discuss our products' ingredients."

"Well, what can you discuss?"

"We offer general consumer information and cleaning tips."

"Okay give me a cleaning tip."

"On what kind of surface?"

"Oh let's see, how about a glass eye?"

"I'm sorry, sir, we don't recommend cleaning glass eyes with Windex." (At this point, we could tell she was starting to get just a wee bit irritated.)

"I tell you what, earlier you said you had 93 cleaning tips for glass; just give me number 93."

"Cleaning tip number 93 says, and I quote, 'For best results, use as directed.'"

"You're kidding, aren't you?"

"No, sir."

"Do you also take comments on your product?"

"Yes, sir, we welcome comments."

"Okay, Windex bites."

"Thank you, I'll be sure to pass it along."

"Have a nice day."

"Thank you for your call."

(Yes, this was a true conversation. If you don't believe it, just give 'em a call.)

SURVEILLANCE CAMERAS RECALLED

The Cody Corp. has recalled 35,000 bank surveillance cameras because as a company spokesman said, "it seemed they were all out of focus." (True)

USA Whenever comment: It's about time! Everytime they show a bank hold-up on TV, I just thought they were showing it through the bottom of a Coke bottle.

This is a non-smoking page. If you must smoke, please step over to page 124.

Made of 'Real Wood'

New Wood Stove

SALE PRICE
Now Only
$39.95
Reg. $19.95

Guaranteed to burn at least 4 hours
Available only in Poland

Bull English Lesson

Sentence One: *It is wrong to kill.* Very good. With 5 words you have stated your position. No one would argue with this statement. Now to the next step . . . logic.

Sentence Two: *People who kill are wrong.* Great. Again all five words are logical, which leads us to the final stage . . . the conclusion.

Sentence Three: Therefore . . . ('therefore' is a great word in English). *Therefore, wrong people must be killed.*

BULL Factoid

If you take something apart and put it back together enough times, eventually you will have two of them.

ever
WONDER
????

Where do people in hell tell people to go?

TEDDY WASN'T READY

Early one morning after a late night date, Teddy Kennedy was driving his girlfriend, Mary Jo, home. "Teddy," Mary Jo said nervously "I think that I might be pregnant." After a moment of thought Teddy answered, "Well, Mary Jo, we'll just have to cross that bridge when we come to it!"

BULL Factoid II

For a man having a sex change operation, the most painful part is having his salary cut in half.

A YANKEE
HALLOWEEN

It won't be long before all the yard apes dress up as monster apes and attack your front door. Let's see how they celebrate Halloween up North.

☛ **Detroit, Michigan** — Up there they call it Devil's Night. It's where all the low-rents get together, dress up real cute, eat a few pieces of candy, and then play that harmless little trick known as "burning the city down." Then all the adults get to dress up as firemen and go try to put it out. I think they should call it "Amoco Unleaded Night."

☛ **Newark, New Jersey** — Most kids in America call it Trick or Treating; in New Jersey, they call it looting. Here all those little future felons dress up in the same clothes. The Newark Wal-Mart even sells them — they're called street gang costumes. Parents are warned to drive slowly in and around business districts where the little lads and lasses will be filling their bags with TVs, microwaves and Nintendo games. The sounds of shattering glass and an occasional "yipee!" when someone finds a Mario 3 or a 2-carat diamond ring all goes to make this a truly festive occasion for all.

BULL
MEDICAL HINT:

You can tell someone is a hypochondriac if they put cough syrup on their pancakes.

JANUARY CALENDAR
Factoids

2

1988: Violence continues to be committed by younger criminals as New Jersey logs it's first skate-by shooting.

7

1990: On this date, Miss Somalia 1990 won their National Swimsuit Contest with measurements of 2-1-2.

8

I got an Energizer Bunny for Christmas. It came with two Duracells.

14

1991: Peace broke out in Miami today, but after several hours of intense negotiations, officials were able to get it under control and the city was able to return to its regularly scheduled violence.

28

Fun Factoid About "Death"
"It it weren't for death, we'd never find a parking spot at the mall."

4 SHORTEST BOOKS IN THUH WORLD

WHAT I MISS MOST ABOUT THE MILLION MAN MARCH

SUCCESFUL PICK-UP LINES THAT INCLUDE THE WORD "MUCUS-MEMBRANE"

HISTORIC MOMENTS IN PUERTO RICAN NAVAL HISTORY

DOUBLEDAY

INTERESTING FACTS ABOUT RAP MUSIC & SOYBEAN SALES

I'LL HAVE A BLACKENED BABY SEAL SANDWICH, SOME MANATEE FINGERS AND 3 BALD EAGLE EGGS SCRAMBLED

McDoodly-doo

Bo Newan

When endangered species are no longer endangered.

The *Love Life* of A **SMILEY** Face

Looking at his naked smiley face girlfriend

Just caught his smiley face girlfriend cheating on him

Just saw both of them get run over by a train

When asked his reaction, he said, "So what?"

Then he found a new smiley face girlfriend and was blissful

She was a pretty smiley face but very bashful

He was love struck!

'Til he found out she was cheatin too.

Boy, was he mad.

So he killed the wretch. It was very satisfying.

Boy, was he shocked when the smiley face police arrested him

And he looked like this when the executioner fired 50,000 volts up his smiley face wazoo.

THUH
END

NOTICE
to our 11 readers

If you are not happy with Thuh Bull, just return the unread portion of your book for a refund and we will be happy to return the unused portion of your money.

We, at the Bull want to thank one special person for his contributions over the years! T. Bubba Bechtol, "America's most loved Bubba" and the funniest man on the planet, has been with us from the beginning. Bubba is a regular on The Nashville Network, humorist, and Country Music's hottest new comedian. Not only will you find much of his "stuff" in this book, but he has contributed jokes, one-liners and headlines over the years, and he is a friend. I thank him and if you like Southern Humor at its best, you will love him! THANKS, BUBBA !!

WIN A BULL T-SHIRT!

If you would like to contribute your funny joke, cartoon, real-life photo or anything humorous to the Bull newspaper and/or next Bull book, please mail it to Thuh Bull, Box 4191, Panama City, FL 32401.

P.S. Be sure to tell us your T-shirt size, 'cause if we print your submission, we will send you our "115% Bull" T-shirt.